NO ZERO DAYS

A FRAMEWORK FOR SUCCESS THROUGH CONSISTENCY

JUSTIN ZEBELL

NO ZERO DAYS

A FRAMEWORK FOR SUCCESS THROUGH CONSISTENCY

JUSTIN ZEBELL

JOIN THE
NO ZERO DAYS
COMMUNITY

Ready to go deeper? Join my email list for:

- Exclusive insights and practical tools

- Speaking event announcements

- Stories from entrepreneurs living with intention

- Early access to workshops and resources

Stay connected at JustinZebell.com

Let's keep building together, one intentional day at a time.

— Justin

DEDICATION

On the darkest day of my life, in July of 2023, my kids saved me. They were none the wiser that day, but it is because of them that I found the path back. So to my youngest three daughters, Anastasia, Chloe, and Claire, I dedicate this book to you. Thank you for teaching me what a life legacy means. When the sun sets on my life, I pray that the philosophies I have adopted will have established a family legacy going forward for you, your children, and your children's children.

Live each day with intention. No Zero Days.

TABLE OF CONTENTS

INTRODUCTION

I AM WHO YOU ARE

You may not know me by name, but I was and am a successful entrepreneur. I don't have a story about selling my first business for $250 million and moving on to start more. I am a grinder. I have fought for everything I have.

I am you. I am an everyday entrepreneur who started a business because I wanted freedom. I wanted to do what I loved: build wealth and live the good life. I thought I had figured it out.

The problem is that we live in an era when the only success stories we celebrate are the overnight ones. The viral, the glamorous, the perfectly packaged. We're constantly looking for the moment—*our* moment. The lightning in a bottle. The podcast interview. The viral clip that makes us the next founder-of-the-minute.

But what happens after the moment passes? What did it cost you to catch it? And what did you sacrifice to keep up?

I earned and I lost, and in the process I learned that what I'd been after was a mirage. It served to teach me what I was *really* after. Armed with that knowledge, rebuilding became easier, is ongoing, and is much more rewarding. I want that for you, too.

WHAT THIS BOOK IS ABOUT

Over the next fourteen chapters I unpack a lifetime of lessons that were delivered to me over a four-year period. They truly transformed who I am, how I lead, and they defined the legacy I want to leave, which is what matters most.

NO ZERO DAYS

I want to share my story complete with the mistakes I made and the lessons I learned so maybe, just maybe, some of you reading this will heed the warning signs and avoid the pitfalls.

But more importantly, in our time together, we'll explore what it means to live with No Zero Days. The premise is simple: Live with intention. Build with purpose. Do something every day, no matter how small, that moves you toward your goals.

The impact is surprisingly huge.

When you live with No Zero Days, you'll learn that you have already arrived. You will live life with intention and turn your day-to-day doldrums into a lifelong adventure. You will live with No Zero Days, and in doing so you will build a meaningful and fulfilling life.

GETTING THE MOST FROM NO ZERO DAYS

Self-awareness is a superpower, and this book is designed to help you harness it. Through honest reflection and practical tools, you'll learn to assess where you are, what's holding you back, and what steps to take next.

The goal is simple but powerful: to help you build a life of No Zero Days—a life defined by daily progress, intentional action, and consistent momentum.

Each chapter explores a deeply personal part of my own journey, marked by ambition, adversity, failure, rebuilding, and growth. You may find parts of your own story mirrored in these experiences.

I don't share these to get your pity or (heaven forbid) as a blueprint, but as proof that change is possible and clarity is earned. I'm including the lessons, tools, and frameworks that helped me to move forward—and can now help you to do the same.

Every section of this book invites you to go one layer deeper into your own development. The exercises are designed to guide you through real reflection and tangible action. They work *if you work them*.

Don't be afraid to stop reading to pause and do the work. You're no stranger to work—the kind that brings in dollars and acclaim.

But the work I'm asking you to do here is deep, shadow work that exposes your vulnerabilities and asks you to explore your true, authentic self. It can get ugly, but it's worth it. Do the work.

I suggest reading the book all the way through once, then returning to the sections that resonate with where you are in your journey. You don't have to solve everything at once—*you just have to keep going.*

This is your moment to commit. To move with purpose. To have No Zero Days. Turn the page and begin.

PART ONE

HOW LEADERS AND ENTREPRENEURS ARE BUILT

What builds a great leader, a great entrepreneur?

Failure.

Self-awareness.

Leaders and entrepreneurs don't find their mettle in easy wins; those are lessons that are learned in failure. Success provides momentum, but failure breeds the resilience, clarity, and wisdom that make success sustainable. Failure is what teaches us the most.

To find the second half of that winning formula, you must understand how YOU specifically are built. What drives you? What drains you? How do each of these contribute to the moxie required to step back into the ring after failure? Are you able to reset quickly? Can you do that with a healthy mindset or is that quick reset derived from the fear of more failure?

Self-awareness is one of today's great underrated superpowers, no matter what phase of life you're in. With it, you have a life hack that deflects anyone else's definition of who you are and who you should be.

In my own story, I had to learn that there was nothing at all wrong with who I was wired to be—that wasn't my problem. However, I was stuck in low gear, even though it looked like I was going places. Armed with that knowledge and the clarity it brought, I was able to find the path to No Zero Days.

CHAPTER ONE

WIRED TO ACHIEVE

If you're like me, you're addicted to the highs of the entrepreneurial journey. Or maybe you're ensconced in a company that rewards your ability to make deals, make things happen, lead the way, and pave the path for others. One way or another, you are a high achiever. It's part of your makeup.

Speaking for myself, the game of business is addicting and rewarding. The way we can take an idea, cobble together a group of people to go from vision to reality, work like crazy, and watch our business or project skyrocket—it's like heroin. We want more. But if those things are true, I am guessing that, like me, your journey has had its share of downsides and crashes, too.

Maybe you figure that it's par for the course, part of the territory of being an entrepreneur or business leader. So, you pick yourself up from the ashes, dust yourself off, and keep on trying. The work will save you. You just have to do more of it.

You are remarkably good at getting the job done. You know how to roll up your sleeves, dig in, and grind until you find the next win. You exhibit remarkable resilience, and you find success, just as you have before.

But the fulfillment you've been chasing feels hollow, so you set out again, convinced that this time you'll finally find the kind of success that feels good deep down.

But before you know it, you're right back where you started, making the same mistakes, working yourself into the ground and wishing it all could be different. Sound familiar?

I bet you know these highs and lows all too well. I know I do. But, if you've picked up this book, I'm betting you're ready to make the shift, like I did, to No Zero Days and true fulfillment. Buckle up, you're in for the ride of a lifetime.

SEEING YOURSELF CLEARLY

I have found that it's helpful to have frameworks that offer tools for self-discovery. When I first discovered it, I found the Enneagram personality model to be incredibly insightful. If you're not familiar with it, the Enneagram is a framework that defines nine core personality patterns, based on what motivates each type and what each type is afraid of.

Like many entrepreneurs and business leaders, I'm a strong Enneagram Type 3—driven by performance, achievement, and a desire to have worth and to be valuable. We're often called "The Achiever."

The Enneagram describes our behavior patterns when we're doing well (and when we're not doing so well) and can be an incredibly useful tool for self-improvement. (This book isn't meant to give you a deep dive into the model, but I've included a few tools and resources in the back of the book if you'd like to explore it further.)

We each have all nine types inside us, so every core fear and corresponding motivating desire will ring somewhat true for us, but we also have a dominant type and it's likely that when you read the following descriptions, one type will ring most true, and will be an indicator of your type. Here are the fears and desires associated with each type.

THE NINE ENNEAGRAMTYPES

TYPE	CORE FEAR	MOTIVATING DESIRE
1	TO BE BAD, WRONG, CORRUPT	TO BE GOOD, RIGHT, AND HAVE INTEGRITY
2	TO BE UNWORTHY OF LOVE AND UNWANTED	TO BE WORTHY OF LOVE AND WANTED
3	TO BE WORTHLESS, TO LACK VALUE	TO HAVE WORTH, TO BE VALUABLE
4	TO BE ORDINARY, TO LACK SIGNIFICANCE	TO BE UNIQUE AND SIGNIFICANT
5	TO BE INCAPABLE OR INCOMPETENT	TO BE CAPABLE AND COMPETENT
6	TO BE WITHOUT SUPPORT OR GUIDANCE	TO HAVE SUPPORT OR GUIDANCE
7	TO BE TRAPPED IN PAIN OR DEPRIVATION	TO HAVE FREEDOM, OPTIONS, POSSIBILITIES
8	TO BE HARMED AND CONTROLLED	TO HAVE AUTONOMY AND BE INDEPENDENT
9	TO BE DISCONNECTED AND CUT OFF	TO BE WHOLE AND UNIFIED

EARLY IMPRINTS

There's a chicken-or-egg question about whether our earliest experiences shape our personalities or if our personalities are the lens through which we filter our earliest experiences, but regardless, we are all shaped by our childhood.

I remember sitting in the corner of my bedroom at my home in Itasca, Texas. I was four years old. Light pierced the dim interior from a corner window, its rays catching the dust on the wood floors and brushing the edge of my bed. But all I could think about was my parents yelling in the next room.

Another fight, which had become an all-too-normal part of my childhood. They were fighting even though they said they loved me.

I sank into the corner, trying to disappear, holding one of my stuffed animals tightly and telling myself, *It will be okay.*

* * *

Years later I'd stand at another window, hoping that my father would show up, and feeling such disappointment when he didn't.

I quickly noticed I received attention and praise when I did well at school or sports. I learned I needed to perform more and perform better. Maybe then he would see me, and I could feel like everything was going to be okay.

Our core wounds present challenges that we face throughout our lives if we don't get a handle on them. And they don't just affect our work life. They're worth examining.

I got married with no model for what a healthy relationship really looked like, but I did have one goal: Don't get divorced.

Noble goal, sure, but anyone can set a goal. The problem came when I didn't have any additional experience, guidance, or know-how to achieve it. That's a recipe for failure.

From the experiences etched into me at age four, I thought I knew the one thing that would keep us together. I told myself, *Don't fight and it will be successful.*

On top of that, the foundational belief that I was not enough drove me to seek approval any way I could.

I don't say any of this to make you feel sorry for me. I'm hoping that by sharing the shadow part of myself you might recognize similar patterns in yourself. Together, we can climb out of the hole.

Everything was about performance and whether I was good enough.

> **I BASED MY IDEA OF WHO I WAS AS A MAN, A LEADER, AND A FATHER ON OTHER PEOPLE'S OPINIONS OF ME, AND I'D BEEN DOING IT SINCE I WAS FOUR YEARS OLD.**

None of my actions came from the knowledge of who I truly was as an individual. How could they? I didn't even know who I was.

I gave myself over to work until I was exhausted and would collapse and emotionally explode, and then I would start that ugly cycle all over again.

I am convinced that my story is one that millions of entrepreneurs and business owners share, though they hide behind the language of "building a business" or "running a company" or "making our numbers" to ignore the hard and very painful truth that they have felt "less than" for a long time.

I was on a never-ending loop. There was no summit. No high peak to reach, look out from, and see that I had succeeded.

Everything I thought would make me feel like I'd succeeded … didn't.

I kept looking, but in trying to find that internal sense of satisfaction a numbness set in. It took time, but I drifted away from myself and slowly morphed into someone I didn't recognize.

There are reasons for that, and we'll get to what the root of the problem was, but first, before we get into my story, let's take a minute to recognize that while we Achievers make mistakes, we also have some pretty amazing strengths.

GIFTS OF THE ACHIEVER

Each of the Enneagram types has different strengths (and, of course, weaknesses), and you may recognize some of yours in the gifts of the Achiever.

Driven: We have an innate desire to achieve and bring projects to completion. And we're good at it. We like to win.

Focused: At our best, we bring remarkable focus and are able to prioritize what matters most and cut through distractions.

Efficient: We don't like to waste time, which we know is a precious resource, so we are skilled at finding the fastest, smartest way to reach a goal.

Adaptive: We can read the room. We can intuitively read people and situations and easily shift our approach to fit the context.

Vision-Oriented: We are future-focused and naturally see opportunities all around us. We are able to paint a picture that inspires others to follow us.

Motivational: We inspire others with our boundless energy, high output, and belief that success is always possible.

Resilient: We can usually bounce back quickly from setbacks and we tend to see obstacles or challenges as fuel rather than brakes.

Charismatic: We are known to build rapport easily and win people's trust with the strength of our presence. We tend to be outgoing and engaging types of people.

Strategic: Our future focus and eye on the prize help us to make smart choices. We instinctively know how to align effort with the outcomes that matter most.

Results-Oriented: We thrive on producing tangible value and measurable progress.

PITFALLS OF PERFORMANCE

Of course, none of us exhibit our healthiest and best behavior 100 percent of the time. The Enneagram describes what each type looks like when it's doing great, when it's average, and when it's not doing well. Most of us fall into average ranges most of the time.

I don't mean to put you in a box. I know that there are tons of things that make you a unique person with great character. But if what I've shared with you so far resonates, there's a good chance we have enough in common that I hope I can help you avoid some of the traps I've fallen into. Furthermore, I promise that this is not a psychology book full of theory and big words. It's an honest exploration of mistakes we Achievers are prone to, and each chapter offers a rung of the ladder that will help you climb out of a dark hole.

Certainly, there are pitfalls for each type. Each of our gifts has a dark side that can throw us into a hole we have trouble climbing out of.

I know from experience just how deep and dark that hole can be. But I did find my way out, and this book is your roadmap to do the same.

ACTION: CELEBRATE YOUR GIFTS

We're going to visit dark and shadowy places in this journey together. It helps to first bolster our thoughts with recognition not just of what we've accomplished, but what we bring to the table.

STEP 1: NAME YOUR NATURAL GIFTS

List five things you do naturally well—think of activities that take you into flow and seem to have low effort but meaningful outcomes.

If unsure, ask three people you trust: "When do you see me at my best? What are my gifts?" Then write down what they say and anything else they've inspired you to recognize in yourself.

Circle the gift that's been most consistent across your life—your through-line strength.

Reflection Prompt

Grab a journal (print or digital) and set up a free-flowing page or document where you can write or type the reflection prompts you'll encounter throughout this book.

Reflecting is best done with free thought and no editing. By the end of this journey, you'll notice a common thread running through your reflections—and that thread may become the connective tissue that ties all your thoughts together.

When did you first notice this gift? How has it shaped your choices or relationships?

STEP 2: SEPARATE GIFTS FROM PERFORMANCE

For each gift, note how it shows up when you're healthy as opposed to when you're hustling for approval.

For example: "Driven" can mean taking disciplined action toward a clear goal (healthy), or it can mean that you've become obsessed with a project to the detriment of everything else in your life (unhealthy).

Choose one boundary this week to keep the gift in its healthiest form. For example, if you're working with "driven," you might set healthy time boundaries on your current passion project to give it progress without having it leak into every aspect of your life. Or you might create a checklist of other important things to complete before diving into a passion project you know will make you lose track of time. If a single project isn't at fault for your "driven" nature, perhaps there's a little workaholism at play here. We'll talk all about that very soon.

STEP 3: REFRAME YOUR STORY

Think of a season when you believed you'd failed.

Now revisit that story through the lens of your gifts. Which strengths showed up, even in the struggle?

Fill in the blank: "That experience showed me that I am ________________."

Why It Matters

Reframing failure as growth is an important step toward wholeness. You're training your brain to see evidence of your resilience, not your failures.

STEP 4: ANCHOR YOUR IDENTITY

Complete these thoughts:

1. "When I am most alive, I am _______________."

2. "When I am most drained, I am _______________."

3. "My worth is not in _______________ but in _______________."

Post your favorite line in a place where you'll see it daily.

CHAPTER TWO

NO ZERO DAYS BEGINS

I've hinted that I've won and lost big, and we'll get to those details soon enough. But in order to begin with the end in mind and help you along on the journey to satisfaction, it helps to know where I ended up after I lost everything and found myself.

A DIFFERENT RHYTHM

It's October in Tennessee. The fall air has settled over the Cumberland Valley, and I sit alone in my apartment.

Alone—a word that once terrified me. Not just the physical solitude, but the deeper meaning: It was *just me, alone.*

I sit here with no distractions, no noise, no one to validate or rescue me. Just my thoughts—unfiltered, unpredictable. And in those thoughts, I often wander to the question of existence itself. *What is the value of me, being alive?*

My thoughts have always been both my greatest triumph and my greatest tragedy—all in the same breath. *One Mississippi.* That's all it takes to shift from grounded to spinning.

But today feels different. It *has* been different.

I woke up with clarity—not from a breakthrough, but from consistency. I slid the patio door open, just as I have every morning this past month, and let the crisp air hit my face. Fall in Tennessee has a way of wrapping around you—less like a season, more like a whisper saying, *You've made it through.*

There's a quiet ritual now. I check on the mums on my porch—they need watering today. Then, on to breakfast.

Some mornings it's a perfect omelet; other mornings it's a scrambled mash. Doesn't matter. What matters is that it starts my day right. While the onions sizzle, I start my coffee.

The mug changes daily. Sometimes it's the one with Walt Whitman's quote—"Be curious, not judgmental." Other times, the quote is from the Ryman Auditorium, arguably my favorite place on earth. "In the absence of words, music speaks." That one hits home. I've lived a life around stages, speakers, music, and moments that became part of my personal soundtrack.

My niche is in the live event industry. My companies have been the driving force behind huge corporate gatherings, high-end experiences, and nationwide touring—you name it. We're the unseen crew behind the curtain, making sure everything goes off without a hitch.

I have built multiple companies, each one better than the last, and I've succeeded in many ways. From the outside, it looked like I had it all. Then I lost it all. Resilience is part of my core being, but no one wants to *have* to be resilient.

This time, I'm sustaining the *better.*

It's darker in the mornings now, as fall deepens, and there's something sacred about this time before the world wakes up. Birds chirp in the courtyard, the curtains sway in rhythm with the breeze, and breakfast simmers with quiet confidence.

Today's result? Scrambled mash. Not perfect—but that's the point. It's not about perfection. It's about intention.

Plate in one hand, coffee in the other, I settle onto the couch next to a book a friend sent me—*The Daily Dad* by Ryan Holiday. Not quite a devotional, but a daily prompt to be more present, more intentional, more *there* for my kids. It's become a vital part of my rhythm. I sip; I eat; I read.

I think the old me would marvel at the intentional slowness of my mornings these days.

Then comes reflection and prayer. Even though it's the most important thing to me, those words still feel foreign. I've taken long breaks from my faith in the past. But here I am.

Some mornings it's just, "Hey, God, it's me, Justin. You might not remember me but…"

Cliché, right? I don't think He minds.

Other times, it's deeper. Raw. Honest. Awkward. Real. It's not perfect—but it's happening.

Then I clean up, take a breath, and look around.

I find that I am happy. Content.

How? How did I find contentment in the ashes of chaos?

It feels like it took a lifetime to find this feeling. And the wildest part? I didn't even know I was looking for it—that I needed it—until everything collapsed.

I'm still driven. Still ambitious. Still on fire to build, create, and lead. But now I carry a different lens. A clearer one. And for the first time in my memory, I can say this without hesitation: *I love who I am.*

No Zero Days is what brought me here.

NO ZERO DAYS ARRIVES

Space and time are funny things. The further you get from an emotional high or low—even one laced with physical pain—the more your brain sands down the edges. Details blur, and you're left with fragments: not the full journey, but the peaks, the final outcome.

In the aftermath of nearly losing everything, I've learned how the mind shields us through quirks like the *peak-end rule* and the *fading affect bias.*

When I look back on the collapse of my business, I don't remember every panic-filled sleepless night or each moment my confidence cracked. Instead, my memory zeroes in on the sharpest spikes of terror and relief—and how the story ultimately concluded.

Meanwhile, the fading affect bias gently dulls the shame, fear, and regret tied to my worst mistakes, softening their sting as months roll by. It's a strange mercy: The further I move from the brink of destruction, the easier it becomes to forget just how reckless some choices were and how close I came to losing it all.

Those distortions are dangerous because they tempt you to repeat the same missteps, having softened their impact in your memory. Or, I could look back and point the finger of blame elsewhere.

But true change was never about anyone other than me. It couldn't be. It can't be for you, either. Because the answer lies within.

As business leaders and family leaders, we have grown accustomed to defining our legacy around stuff and titles, and in doing so we never truly find out who WE are. Contentment is found when you begin to figure that out.

For months after my crash, I asked myself: *How do I follow this intense drive to succeed, which is woven into my DNA, without living perpetually on the edge of a cliff?*

I worried my story might simply replay itself over and over—different stage, same plot, no real progress. This was the new question burning inside me.

How do I move with intensity and purpose without falling into the same traps over and over again?

I looked for inspiration in people who'd walked the path ahead of me. And that's how I stumbled across Jesse Itzler on social media. I barely knew who he was at the time. But the more I listened, the more his words resonated with my own search for something more sustainable and real.

I remember the moment I first read these three simple words:

No Zero Days.

He often used the phrase with his kids as they chased hard goals.

Those words stopped me in my tracks.

No Zero Days.

Curious, I dug deeper and found the original post from 2013 in a Reddit thread now known as "Ryan's Rules."[1] The essence of "No Zero Days" was beautifully simple: Do something every day—no matter how small—that moves you toward your goals.

On the surface, it sounded like yet another self-help slogan, another motivational fad destined to fade away like so many before it.

But for some reason, it stuck.

---

[1] https://www.reddit.com/r/NonZeroDay/comments/1qbxvz/the_gospel_of_ury-ans01_helpful_advice_for_anyone/

"Ryan" described a No Zero Day as a day in which you take any sort of action toward your big goal. It's 11:57 p.m. and you haven't taken action toward your biggest goal? You find a small thing and you do it. You do it for your future self.

In the morass of an ugly crash, depression and lethargy can make it so that taking even one action can be incredibly difficult and hugely rewarding. Take one small step every day as a bare minimum.

Once you have momentum, you'll naturally find that some days become huge No Zero Days, in which you accomplish way more than one thing. After all, you're an Achiever. You're built to make things happen.

That definition was a starting point for me. No Zero Days. I could do one thing … but how did I know what my biggest goal was and if it was worth chasing? I kept circling back to the question:

What is a No Zero Day for me?

WHAT IS A NO ZERO DAY?

For months, as I grappled my way out of the darkest hole, I wrestled with that question both in my mind and in my journal. *What does it really mean to live with No Zero Days? Can I even do it? Can anyone?*

And then one morning, in the quiet of my journaling and prayer time, I asked God to help keep my heart anchored to the things that truly matter. I knew what they were without a doubt: my faith, my kids, my family, and my friends.

And that's when it struck me with crystalline clarity.

No Zero Days means taking action with **intention**. It means achieving **contentment**. It means easier realignment when I feel the drift because I know my **priorities**, and I use my energy toward them *first.*

I grabbed my pen and scribbled out my three guideposts. It looked like this:

- Faith

- Family and friends

- My entrepreneurial passions

And then everything else.

It was the complete inverse of how I'd lived over the past decade.

And it was monumental.

Not because it was some grand plan or a color-coded calendar. Not because it was a checklist or a ten-step program. But because it was simple.

I didn't need a hundred self-help books to help me figure out my life.

If I kept my first two priorities in place—because they are what I live *for*—then I could go full throttle on everything else: my business, my passions, and my big goals.

And that's how I fell in love with three simple words.

No Zero Days.

If you can't define your purpose in your own life, then you can't define it for your family or your business. Without a deeper *what* and *why* behind your vision, you will struggle to find a team that truly follows you, be that at home or in the office.

You're probably thinking, *That's it? Focus on my pillars? Move the needle just a little? That's supposed to change everything? It sounds too simple.*

I get it. You might feel like you need to burn it all down, reinvent yourself from scratch, follow a twenty-step system, and attend a psychedelic experience in order to rebuild from the ashes.

But you don't. You just need alignment. When your pillars are clear and your drive kicks in, and it will, you'll be moving with purpose. Every step forward will bring you closer to who you are meant to be and what you really want.

No Zero Days.

These words are my compass. They are a daily reminder that progress is about small, deliberate steps forward, every single day, *with full intentionality* behind each of those steps. They were my path out of the darkness.

ACTION: IDENTIFY YOUR PILLARS

A triangle forms a very stable base, and so three pillars are what we rest our No Zero Days on. I can't tell you what your three pillars are: That's completely personal. Your pillars may have nothing in common with mine. You get to decide what they are.

You may already know what your three pillars are and in what order they fall. If that's the case, fantastic—write them down.

But it may take you a little time or effort to discover or decide what is most important to you for the long haul.

If your pillars don't immediately leap out at you, fully formed and obvious, that's okay. Spend some time in creative exploration and walk through the following four steps.

STEP 1: GET QUIET ENOUGH TO HEAR YOURSELF

Set aside ten minutes a day in silence—no phone, no music, no distractions.

Let clarity rise on its own.

REFLECTION

Grab that journal and jot down the answers to these questions:
When was the last time you felt true peace?
What were you doing?
More importantly, what *wasn't* present in that moment? No filter. No editing. No wrong answers.

STEP 2: NAME WHAT TRULY MATTERS

List five things or people that give life meaning for you beyond achievement—faith, family, friendship, purpose, creativity, service, etc.

Circle the three that feel foundational. These are your pillars.

If you're struggling to pick three because you want to make sure you've explored all your options or you aren't quite sure what to call them, I've put together a list of possibilities for you to consider.

I suggest you circle any of them that resonate with you and then, if you circle more than three, take the time to truly understand which three are the most important to you.

You might ask yourself what it would feel like either to live with that pillar as your guidepost or, on the flip side, what it would be like to live without it as a compass. How would your life change for better or worse?

RELATIONSHIPS AND COMMUNITY PILLARS

Family. Prioritizing time and love for those closest to you.

Friends. Investing in deep, supportive friendships.

Romantic partnership or marriage. Nurturing a loving, committed relationship.

Children. Guiding, protecting, and enjoying your kids' lives.

Extended family. Maintaining bonds with parents, siblings, and relatives.

Mentorship (giving or receiving). Learning from others or helping them grow.

Community service. Serving and improving your local community.

Belonging/tribe. Being part of a group where you feel accepted.

Hospitality. Creating welcoming spaces for others.

Legacy/ancestry. Honoring where you come from and what you pass on.

PERSONAL GROWTH AND INNER LIFE PILLARS

Faith/spirituality. Connecting with a higher power or meaning.

Personal integrity. Living true to your values and promises.

Wisdom. Seeking understanding and discernment.

Learning/education. Expanding your knowledge and skills.

Curiosity. Staying open and inquisitive about life.

Self-expression. Sharing your inner world through words, art, or action.

Emotional resilience. Building the capacity to handle life's ups and downs.

Personal growth or self-mastery. Continually evolving as a person.

Self-understanding. Taking time to think deeply and understand yourself.

Authenticity. Showing up as your true self, without masks.

HEALTH AND WELL-BEING PILLARS

Physical health. Maintaining strength, energy, and vitality.

Exercise/movement. Keeping your body active and flexible.

Nutrition. Fueling your body with nourishing foods.

Rest/sleep. Prioritizing recovery and relaxation.

Mental health. Supporting your emotional and psychological well-being.

Mindfulness/meditation. Staying present and aware in the moment.

Nature connection. Spending time outdoors and appreciating the natural world.

Balance/harmony. Creating equilibrium between all areas of life.

Vitality/energy. Choosing activities that make you feel alive.

Safety. Ensuring physical and emotional security for yourself and others.

WORK AND ACHIEVEMENT PILLARS

Career advancement. Growing and succeeding professionally.

Entrepreneurship. Building and running your own business.

Mastery of craft. Becoming exceptional at what you do.

Financial security. Creating stability and freedom through money.

Wealth-building. Growing long-term financial abundance.

Recognition. Valuing acknowledgment for your work and contributions.

Innovation. Creating new ideas, products, or ways of thinking.

Achievement. Setting and reaching meaningful goals.

Excellence. Doing your work to the highest standard.

Influence. Inspiring and impacting others positively.

CREATIVITY AND EXPRESSION PILLARS

Art. Making or appreciating beauty through visual mediums.

Music. Creating or enjoying music that moves you.

Writing. Expressing yourself through stories, essays, or journaling.

Storytelling. Sharing narratives that connect and inspire.

Performance. Expressing yourself through acting, dance, or speaking.

Design/aesthetics. Crafting pleasing and functional environments.

Invention. Creating something entirely new.

Play. Engaging in fun, spontaneous activities.

Adventure. Seeking out new and exciting experiences.

Imagination. Dreaming big and exploring ideas beyond the ordinary.

CONTRIBUTION AND SERVICE PILLARS

Leadership. Guiding and inspiring others toward a shared goal.

Service to others. Helping meet the needs of those around you.

Advocacy/activism. Standing up for causes you believe in.

Volunteering. Giving time and energy to help your community.

Justice/fairness. Working to make life equitable for all.

Teaching. Sharing your knowledge and helping others grow.

Environmental stewardship. Protecting and caring for the earth.

Philanthropy. Giving resources to meaningful causes.

Generosity. Offering your time, talent, or treasure freely.

CONNECTION AND EXPERIENCE PILLARS

Travel. Exploring new places and cultures.

Exploration. Trying new activities or perspectives.

Wonder. Allowing yourself to feel awe and curiosity.

Shared experiences. Creating memories with others.

Celebration/joy. Honoring life's big and small milestones.

Intimacy. Cultivating deep emotional and physical closeness with others.

Belonging. Feeling seen, valued, and connected.

Connection with animals. Caring for and enjoying animals.

Cultural appreciation. Learning about and honoring diverse traditions.

Rituals/traditions. Creating meaningful repeated practices.

STABILITY AND STRUCTURE PILLARS

Security. Establishing safety and predictability.

Home/sanctuary. Creating a safe, nurturing environment.

Order/organization. Bringing structure to your life.

Simplicity/minimalism. Focusing on what truly matters.

Routine/rhythm. Finding steadiness through habits.

Preparedness. Being ready for challenges.

Discipline. Following through on commitments.

Reliability. Being trustworthy and consistent.

Tradition. Preserving and honoring meaningful practices.

Stewardship. Taking good care of resources entrusted to you.

HIGHER PURPOSE AND MEANING PILLARS

Hope. Believing in a better future.

Faith in humanity. Trusting in people's goodness.

Spiritual connection. Seeking meaning beyond yourself.

Contribution. Making a positive difference in the world.

Legacy. Leaving something meaningful behind.

Purpose. Living with clear intention and meaning.

Transcendence. Experiencing life beyond the everyday.

Calling. Responding to what feels uniquely yours to do.

Vision. Imagining and pursuing a better future.

PERSONAL ANCHORS PILLARS

Humor. Finding and sharing laughter.

Beauty. Surrounding yourself with and creating beauty.

Adventure/athleticism. Seeking thrills and physical challenge.

Gardening/cultivating. Growing plants or tending the earth.

Storytelling with family history. Preserving and sharing heritage.

Intellectual challenge. Solving problems and expanding your mind.

Innovation in technology. Exploring and creating new tech solutions.

Playfulness. Keeping a sense of fun and lightness.

Courage. Acting bravely despite fear.

Freedom. Living according to your own values and choices.

* * *

STEP 3: PUT YOUR PILLARS IN ORDER

After choosing your three guiding pillars, rank them by importance. There is no right or wrong here. You may have more than three pillars and that is perfectly fine.

Why It Matters

When you are clear on what your pillars are, peace replaces chaos—and it becomes easy for you to know what deserves your "yes." Time is your most important resource, and when you use the guidance of the pillars to allocate yours, your life will move into alignment.

STEP 4: CREATE YOUR DAILY ANCHOR

Choose one small action that honors your top pillar and implement it daily: It might be to say a prayer, state your gratitude, or send a loving message to your kids.

Consistency beats intensity.

* * *

I don't expect my pillars to change, but as your life evolves, yours might. Revisit this exercise whenever you sense that your pillars no longer inspire you to take action.

PART TWO

THE WAR WITHIN

It's all well and good for me to tell you I've got it all together now. But, as I've already admitted, that hasn't always been the case. Truth be told, I'm still a work in progress, and I expect to be for the rest of my life. I've made more than my share of mistakes.

Hindsight being as accurate as it is, I now see clearly how adrift I was from my pillars ... and how devastating the consequences were.

In this section we're going to explore the ways we hide from the world and from ourselves, figure out how to let go of the masks we wear (or at least identify them), and to start to find the authentic version of ourselves that the world deserves as much as we do.

We'll explore some of the ways we betray ourselves when we don't have the No Zero Days mentality, even—*especially*—when we're riding high on a mountain of successes, bringing home win after win after win.

You'd think that would mean we've made it. But if we're living without the intention of No Zero Days, our successes might be so hollow that we only feel emptiness when we achieve them.

Maybe you're feeling like you're crushing it. You don't need guidance or help. You're a winner. You're the queen or king of the world. You have the golden touch. Your bank account is growing fatter and fatter, and everything you want is within reach.

I know all too well: That's when you need the calibration of No Zero Days the most.

CHAPTER THREE

WE WEAR THE MASK

THE WAR BEHIND THE SMILE

You're riding high, leading with energy and excitement, bringing home the wins … but no one is celebrating with you at home. You've somehow grown distant from the ones you love the most.

You could offer a master class in compartmentalization. One part of you shows up to work every day—polished, high-functioning—and that version of you delivers results that make people applaud.

You have great camaraderie with your team. You're all smiles, laughter, and energy at work. But on the way home, the deadness sets in. You close a record-setting quarter but ask yourself, *Is this it?* You hit the stage, crush your pitch, then sit alone in a hotel room, feeling hollow.

The war within is like mental tennis. In one world you feel like you can do no wrong: Your accomplishments are *everything*. You are a winner. Hands down, no questions asked.

But in the other world you find yourself scrambling to stay in the game. The ref doesn't think you're even good enough to be on the court, and you're constantly late to the ball. There is no timeout. No crowd cheering the effort. Just you, swinging in silence against yourself. And it sucks. And it hurts. And you may not even be aware that you're at war because you're sure the next win is just around the corner, *and it will save you.*

You'll never let anyone see that pain, though, so you put on the mask, the one with a smile that says *everything's great*, and you barrel on.

Here's the truth: The war never ends unless you acknowledge it exists.

Most people never do. They keep performing. Keep producing. Keep pretending. Stopping long enough to examine the wounds means admitting the pain is real.

But the cost of ignoring the war is steep—burnout, bitterness, and eventually, a crash. If left unchecked, you become a high-functioning shell, performing the role of "successful person" while privately questioning what it's all for and if it's even worth it.

If left further unchecked, your confidence and your zealous chase of the next win are almost guaranteed to bring their own disastrous results.

This chapter is about learning how to see the war within, because you don't have to exist as a lonely and unfulfilled person underneath the success. But until you acknowledge you're fighting this internal war, you'll never step off the battlefield.

IS THIS IT?

Is this it? Three words. Eight letters. One haunting question.

This phrase is often marked with disappointment, unmet expectations, and a loud but unvoiced sigh.

As children, we could wear our disappointment on our faces. As adults in corporate America, we swallow it, push it down. We're told something must be wrong with us if we're not grateful for everything we have.

Don't be disappointed.

Be grateful for what you have.

Say thank you.

Be polite.

You know you're the lucky one.

Not everyone gets this opportunity.

… and the list goes on …

It's nauseating, isn't it? But we smile, silence that internal voice, and repeat those phrases to ourselves until we can believe them, at least for one more day.

Is this it?

Sigh.

Maybe you've asked that question, but then you did what you do best: got back to work.

I get it. It's understandable. Life is filled with ups and downs, and just when you think you can't deal with any more downs, you get an up—and it's enough of an adrenaline shot to push you forward and allow you to ignore that quiet but enormous question: *Is this it?*

Here's the thing—if you don't try to answer that question, the invisible weight only gets heavier.

Is this it?

It doesn't shout. It lingers.

It echoes in boardrooms after the big pitch.

It echoes when you pull into your driveway and you celebrate your success with more *stuff*. It settles into your chest when the applause fades. It shows up in quiet hotel rooms, long drives, and the spaces between milestones.

If you've ever asked yourself that question, it's a sign that your calibration is off. You're chasing victories, but they are hollow for you because they aren't in alignment with your true desires.

Is this it? is a call for you to get real with yourself. If you glossed over choosing your three pillars in Chapter Two, but you're hearing this little voice of discontentment, revisit that exercise now.

If you've chosen your pillars and you're still hearing that voice, it's time for a recalibration. You'll want to examine your life and see if you're truly living in alignment with your core values. I will share with you how I did that in Chapter Twelve.

FA-LA-LA AND KEEP SMILING

In the early part of my career, I had the privilege of working in music with some of the most talented people in Nashville. I've lived the dream of touring the country and the world. I spent the better part of twenty years as a production manager and then as a tour manager.

What is a tour manager, you ask? I was the conductor, and the orchestra size changed from tour to tour, but it was my job to keep every aspect of the tour on time and ensure that everyone played their part—from the venue to the crew to the artists and even the fans. The buck stopped with me and I loved it. I loved that pressure, and, honestly, I loved the thrill of controlling the rhythm everyone moved to.

My career has been filled with pinnacle moments: From premier events at The Kennedy Center, to being one of a few hundred people present for First Lady Barbara Bush's ninetieth birthday party, to concerts and shows in arenas and venues around the world, I've been blessed with so many great experiences.

My favorite experience would come—and still comes—at the end of each year as we celebrate Christmas, as one of my longtime friends and clients continues the longest running live show residency at the Ryman Auditorium, known as the "Mother Church of Country Music."

By day I felt like a hero as my team and I worked to give others a great Christmas experience, but at night I'd go home to a dark place where I felt like a failure—as a partner and a father.

I was desperate for an approval I could no longer find at home. I had tried for years to make the relationship work, but it's exhausting to keep pouring energy into a bottomless tank of a relationship that never seems to meet your standards or your partner's. We can only do that for so long.

I got good at avoiding the darkness. I was always onto the next thing. You probably know this feeling. We're entrepreneurs and leaders. The drive is in our blood. The work is always there to do.

I specifically recall one December—my team and I were on the brink of a breakout year when the calendar flipped to January. Over the previous years, I'd been fortunate enough to have a bit of what you'd call the Midas touch, and this particular year we were closing out on a high.

Our trajectory was going to change everything that was missing in my life (or so I told myself). So, I did what many of us are so good at. I leaned into the work, compartmentalized, and went through what had become lifeless motions of Christmas.

Though I didn't understand how thoroughly my need to be liked was manifesting itself at the time, now that my goals are in alignment with my pillars, I can see how desperately I wanted all of the outward trappings of success. I thought once I had them, I'd finally feel like I'd made it.

My need to be seen as successful, as accomplished, as "the guy who made it," manifested itself in stretching my family financially so that we could live in the "it" neighborhood.

And as much as I was a master compartmentalizer, my need to be liked manifested itself in my career like a cancer.

But at the time I thought I was on the right track. Everything looked perfect from the outside. My mask was firmly in place. I didn't dare let anyone know how ugly everything was on the inside, especially myself.

The brutal truth is that I missed so many important moments with my family while I remained out of alignment. The world happened around me and to me—and I watched it all from an isolated, numb point of view. For too long I was a man alone, in the middle of a lake with no shore in sight.

HERO AT WORK

In early January, I was driving out to a beautiful resort in Alabama for our biggest staff retreat yet. Even though the question *Is this it?* had grown louder, I was riding high that day.

I lived for drives like this, out in nature. It was here where I found peace. Watching the sun dance off the winter fields while moving effortlessly down a two-lane road in the American South … it was deeply soul satisfying to me.

I remember passing trailer parks and areas that were more run-down, shaking my head and thinking, *Gosh, who lives like this?* and, *I can't believe this is all so close to such a nice resort.*

In my mind I'd left behind the life of poverty I'd known growing up for good. I was someone who now got to enjoy the good life. *I'm one of the lucky ones,* I told myself and, *Not everyone gets this kind of opportunity*. My company was on the verge of its biggest year yet.

I turned onto the winding road that led up to the resort. Everything I saw was perfectly manicured, elegant, and high end. I thought, *This is appropriate. This is the life I want.* I took in the beauty of the landscape while simultaneously wondering what it would take for me to own something just like it.

I pulled up to the resort in my luxury SUV, and the valet greeted me by name. I felt like a big deal. I was a big deal. And I liked that feeling. Who wouldn't?

We kicked off that evening with an opening reception. I loved our team. I loved investing in them. While I certainly craved that feeling of having arrived, I also cared deeply about their success. They were *my* team. I knew their strengths and where they found joy. I was looking forward to what would come from the weekend's collaboration. This was the first retreat we'd invited our employees' spouses to so they could share in the fun.

Me? I was alone and I am sure it was hurtful to my spouse that I didn't even extend an invitation. But who I was at work was not who I was at home. I couldn't imagine those two versions of myself existing in the same room.

I looked around the reception and felt such happiness with what I saw and who was there. From the golfing and horseback riding to an unbelievable mountain-top seafood boil, we were celebrating and living life as a strong community.

The retreat was a success. We had great sessions during the day and were calculating the launch of another division within our agency. Everything—*and I mean everything*—was going right. We were going places. We were going to take the year by storm.

We incubated some really cool ideas. I formalized the full-time addition of a long-time consultant to our team, and we were on the verge of landing the largest single contract we'd ever won, all while wrapping up concepts for the world's largest search engine.

I threw a music jam session in the car all the way home. I was made for this, and all of the hard work I'd put in over the last decade was starting to pay off. The following weeks we were all in high gear, our business was set to fly like never before, and we were working hard to make that happen. I spent a lot of time at work. I was going to make everyone's dreams come true. I was going to find "it."

* * *

In February I started to hear rumblings about some airborne virus coming out of Asia. The word *pandemic* was being used, but we'd all heard it before and it had always been just a blip on the radar. In my recent memory Ebola and the avian flu had come and gone with hardly an impact on regular American lives. Still …

I knew I was thinking ahead, and maybe it's the Boy Scout in me, but I have always loved being prepared. I made a phone call to one of our team members, based on a gut feeling.

"Hey, do you remember that streaming platform we built for those events in 2017?" I asked.

They remembered.

"Great," I told them. "I don't think we'll need it, but just in case this virus thing turns into something, let's dust that off and create a branded demo. Just in case. I'm not sure what's coming; you never know."

I hung the phone up and put my attention back on our upcoming event in Colorado. I had no idea how important that phone call would become or the impact it would ultimately have on me even five years later.

* * *

LISTEN TO YOUR GUT

As entrepreneurs we like to use our heads, make rational choices, look at the numbers, and trust that work will make all the difference.

It may be just as important to listen to our gut instincts and follow up on them. When you follow your gut, you're tapping into a complex, biologically wired feedback system that connects your brain and body.

The gut has its own neural network, often called the "second brain," which communicates constantly with your central nervous system through the vagus nerve. What feels like instinct is your body synthesizing years of subconscious pattern recognition, emotional memory, and internal sensory input in milliseconds, faster than your rational mind can process.

In high-stakes or uncertain environments, like deciding whether to pivot a business or take a risk during chaos (hello, COVID), gut instinct acts as a rapid-response filter for action. It's your body's way of helping you survive and make decisions when time or data is limited. The best leaders don't just trust their gut blindly. They've learned to listen to it because it's often *the first place* their experience shows up.

It may be the best source in determining what voices you hear and more importantly, which of those voices you will listen to most.

What I mean by that is your gut is acting as a filter and a guide, helping you to notice important messages. It just might be the one whispering, *Is this it?*

* * *

WHEN THE WORLD TILTED

A few weeks later our team boarded flights bound for Colorado. The rumblings of some kind of disease were real now, but there were still a lot of questions surrounding whether it would amount to anything at all. The consensus was that whatever this disease-of-the-week was, it would be short-lived and life would carry on just as it always had.

Still. Good leaders plan for contingencies. I landed in Colorado and called my banker, an outstanding individual who understood small business partnerships. We discussed the worst-case scenario. We chatted about our company's needs, our monthly overhead, and whether we were in a position to receive immediate support from the bank if we needed it.

Just before we hung up, he said, "I'm sure this won't amount to much … but if it does, we'll support you through whatever's needed."

That was the first week of March 2020.

As they had so many times before, that week our team delivered an excellent event to a ballroom brimming with more than 1,200 guests. Little did we know what a swan song that would be.

That Friday, when I joined several of our clients' executives on a shuttle for the airport, the tone of the conversation had dramatically changed. It seemed it was no longer a question of *if* the pandemic was going to affect us, but *when*. Sickness was spreading like wildfire wherever it landed. People were starting to take notice and a quiet dread settled over that shuttle.

On the flight home I began to face the reality of what might be coming. That Monday I had discussions with my team about the events we had booked for the next month. Could any of them be impacted by this virus thing?

I came away from those discussions feeling prepared. The impact to our business seemed like it would be negligible, a bump in the road. And it wouldn't last more than a few weeks, tops.

SECURE YOUR MASK IN CASE OF EMERGENCY

As the potential crisis that was COVID continued to unfold, the question *Is this it?* was pushed to the background. There was no time for it. I could ignore that quiet voice even as it grew louder, because to pay attention to it required me to confront some very inconvenient truths—and there was *so much work to be done*. I used work as a shield from the hard truths I needed to face.

Answering the question *Is this it?* can be as much about moving away from something painful as it is about moving toward something better. Here's the kicker: Nine out of ten times, to find the answer to the question *Is this it?* you will see that the single biggest roadblock to the answer is the person looking back at you in the mirror.

"I don't have time for this now," is one of the stories we tell ourselves when we choose to ignore that voice asking: *Is this it?* We'd rather stay shallow, tread that hamster wheel, and dance to the people-pleasing beat than slow down and do the deep introspection necessary for true happiness.

ACTION: ASSESS YOUR MASKS

I am not the first person, nor will I be the last, who writes about the masks we wear as humans. Some of us refer to them as multiple hats or personas, but regardless of what you call them, they almost always hide us from authentic behavior.

We certainly have various roles to play in life, from spouse to partner to business leader and so on, but we are at our best when those roles are undergirded by our authentic self.

Assessing your masks is about uncovering what you are hiding in order to take on the role of a certain persona. Here's a hint: It is the secret parts of you that no one knows or that you think no one knows. And it is exhausting to constantly hide this part of yourself, the most real part.

If you feel as if your various worlds can never coexist in the same room, then you need to take some time to assess what masks you're wearing and how it impacts those closest to you. Start here with these four prompts:

STEP 1: NAME THE MASK OR MASKS

Write down the version of yourself you show when you're "on."

What does that persona project—confidence, humor, control, perfection, positivity?

WHAT FEAR ARE YOU HOLDING ON TO BECAUSE YOU BELIEVE IT'S PROTECTING YOU?

STEP 2: SPOT THE SPLIT

Create three columns: *Work You, Home You,* and *You When No One Is Watching.*

Write three to five words under each heading, then examine your lists and take note of any contradictions.

Awareness begins when you see the gap between your public rhythm and private reality.

STEP 3: OBSERVE YOUR TENDENCIES

As you move through the week ahead, take note of which persona or mask you put on the most and what situations or people are triggering you the most.

CHAPTER FOUR

ANTI-FRAGILE

I hope it's clear now that I was a split man, living two lives. And with turmoil bubbling under the surface, all of that was personal. I kept it separate from work.

And what was in front of me was a supreme challenge. I could let it flatten me. Or I could rise to meet it.

I'd bet you're not someone who would give up without a righteous fight. I'm not either. Our personality type might have its challenges, but it definitely has its gifts, and our ability to rise to the challenge is one of them.

THE DAY THE WORLD STOPPED

We all remember where we were when it hit us—this disease wasn't just media hype. This was real. Something none of us fully understood was unfolding, and the world shut down. Not just in some distant part of the globe. Not in a land far away. Right here. My city. My neighborhood.

The NBA suspended its season. The NCAA tournament was canceled. Schools closed. Offices sent employees home to work from quickly cobbled-together remote offices. Children attended school from home—in isolation. In a matter of hours, everything we thought was immovable became uncertain. The world grew silent as planes were grounded and the streets were empty of cars and people. The routines we relied on disappeared. Life as we knew it was called into question.

For a company like ours, whose main source of revenue was live events, the reality landed fast and hard. In just four days, we lost $11 million in contracts.

We weren't a large company, but this was supposed to be our breakout year. And suddenly, it all stopped. One cancellation phone call after another landed relentlessly, like body blows.

On Friday afternoon, March 20, I took the final call—our sole remaining client pulled the last piece of business we'd had remaining on the table for the foreseeable future.

I set the phone down and couldn't breathe. I was alone in the "home office" I'd created in the basement. I pushed my chair back, found the darkest corner of the room, and crawled into it with a pillow. I stayed there for an hour or more, trying to inhale, trying to quiet the chaos running through my mind.

Why didn't I plan for this? How could I not be prepared for an apocalyptic event? Funny now, maybe. But back then, it wasn't. No one was prepared.

The entire live events industry was crushed. Over 12 million jobs lost globally in a matter of weeks. In that moment all I could feel was the suffocating weight of personal responsibility.

My family. My team. Their families. Their fears. I carried them all. We were all in it together, but the isolation of the pandemic made it feel like we were each on an island, staring out into the unknown. Every expert had a theory. Every theory was wrong.

That hour in the basement felt like an eternity. I wanted to go to sleep and wake up when it was all over.

THE ECHO OF *IS THIS IT?*

Alone in the basement I let out the emotions I would never let anyone see. There were tears. Rage. Helplessness. Shame. Every emotion and every four-letter word came out.

As afternoon turned to twilight and then to night, I went upstairs, hugged my kids, and headed back down to sleep alone in the basement.

Maybe it would all go away the next day. Maybe this was just a blip.

But something deeper was unraveling. The question I'd been avoiding suddenly had plenty of space and breathing room to rear its ugly head.

Is this it?

Is this what all the late nights, the sacrifices, and the hard climbs had been for? Standing at the edge of collapse, I was unsure if I even wanted to try to save what I'd built. *How could that even be true?* But it was.

Is this it?

That question shook something in me. It wasn't just about business. It was about my identity. My worth and my self-worth. I'd spent years building an image of resilience—the guy who could outwork, outlast, outclimb anyone. But in that basement, stripped of all certainty, I became a little kid again, huddled in the corner like I was four.

If I can't perform my role, what do I do to keep everyone from leaving me?

And with that came the scariest question of all: *How do I prove I still matter when everything I was good at is gone?*

I didn't know the answer. But I knew that work had always saved me. The two weeks that followed are a blur in my memory. I filled my days with tasks just to feel useful.

The world was shut down, but I created motion to mask the stillness I couldn't bear. I drove the Natchez Trace aimlessly, just to escape the walls of my house—and the loud questions in my mind.

I missed moments I'll never get back. I wasn't present for my kids. I wasn't present for myself. I withdrew out of fear and unspoken shame—the shame of failure, and the realization that nothing I did could stop a global pandemic.

THE CHOICE WE FACE

In those empty days, the whisper became a shout—and in that rising noise, I found myself straining for something to hold onto. That's when the flicker appeared. It wasn't clarity or even a direction yet. Just the faintest glimmer of light in a storm of unknowns.

I knew I couldn't stay in my cave forever. I had to go perform. Win everyone's approval. Save the day. That's what I was built for and I wasn't going to let everyone down. That's why they liked me. Right?

I had to pick myself up, dust myself off, and find a way through.

THE 14 PERCENT

I remember the day everything shifted for the better. That morning, I was worn thin. The prior weeks had been filled with crash courses in something called Zoom, tough calls with our finance team, and difficult conversations about cash flow, layoffs, and survival.

I sat down, exhausted, and searched for something—anything—that could give me hope (or at least offer a momentary escape). I picked up my phone and started scrolling. Fast. Past the fearmongering. Past the bad news. Past the noise. And then, amid the blur, something caught my attention: a headline.

The article I stumbled on shared two points that changed everything. First, it reminded me that global economic disruption isn't rare. In fact, in the United States, major events hit roughly every ten years.

We had 9/11 in 2001. The banking and housing crisis in 2008. And now—this. Yes, if you're counting, we have five years or less before our next disruption.

Oh.

The older I get, the more I realize just how often these disruptions shake up everyone's lives.

Each of these events creates a profound shift in what's "normal." We never return to normal as we knew it. Change is the only constant.

The article went on to say that out of five hundred companies surveyed, 86 percent of them chose to hold the status quo, lay off staff, batten down the hatches, ride out the storm, and wait for a return to normal. Which we've just established will never really come around again. So, these companies are slower to react to our new reality.

BUT 14 percent of companies use this time of disruption to reinvent themselves. They invest in new tech, new methodologies, and see it as a time to reinvent themselves, to be agile and adapt to the new normal, and, even better, help to define it.

This was the moment of inspiration I needed. After weeks in a fog, I had something to latch onto. I had a goal. My company was going to be one of the elite few. That was it. We were going to be part of the 14 percent, not the 86 percent.

I had no idea how, but I accepted the challenge implicit in the article. Everything had to start with me. I had to look in the mirror and end the whining.

That article became a kind of mentor to me. A gut check. It snapped me out of damage control and reignited the idea of creative leadership. We wouldn't just survive—we'd rebuild better.

RALLYING THE TEAM

The early days of the pandemic gave all of us a strange gift: time to cocoon, reassess, and rediscover. We sent our team home like everyone else, leaned hard into Zoom, and built new rhythms.

Community mattered more than ever. And in that shared pause, something powerful began to happen. We leaned into togetherness—delivering meals to each other's homes, hosting watercolor painting happy hours over video calls, and creating daily content just to keep each other's spirits lifted. It was messy, honest, and deeply human.

That spirit carried into our work. Ideas flowed. Titles didn't matter. Egos disappeared. Eight of us locked in, problem-solving without borders. It was raw and refreshing.

We were moving. We were innovating. We were the 14 percent.

The call I'd made in February about reinvigorating our streaming platform served as the genesis for our new endeavor. We worked with that partner to showcase a virtual platform to our clients. The little demo we created was proof of concept that grew into what would become a company called JoinIn.

JoinIn was a virtual platform designed to create virtual events that felt familiar. These virtual environments replaced in-person events, providing engagement between attendees that were hundreds if not thousands of miles apart. We created custom virtual convention spaces that connected us all in the midst of the pandemic. Our live events were like full-scale television productions broadcast into home offices across the globe.

The demo kept conversations going. It reminded our clients that we were still here, still innovating, still solving problems. In a world of uncertainty, it showed we were figuring things out.

But even in the midst of momentum, deeper questions lingered.

The question *Is this it?* had been interrupted by my new initiative, but not erased. I didn't have the space to deal with it then … or so I told myself. But it kept showing up. Quietly at first, then louder. The numbness had cracked. The fog had thinned. And with it came clarity, pain, and a hard truth: Inaction would have destroyed our business, and the inaction ruling the rest of my compartmentalized life was destroying me.

WHAT'S IN A NAME?

Naming JoinIn taught me one of the most humbling lessons of my career. It was a marker to listen to those you have surrounded yourself with more than your own voice in your head.

As entrepreneurs, we are often left to our own devices after the nine-to-five clock shuts off, and we make so many decisions on our own that we can lose sight of the value of input from others. This was a lesson I learned during the pandemic but certainly failed to heed later.

We followed the lead of pioneers like 37signals and Basecamp—build only what's necessary, ship it, and improve later. Our first event launched on the platform in July. Our second? It was a global event. We were back in motion.

I was admittedly in a speed-over-perfection mindset. You may often find yourself in business in that mindset, and I champion that approach. Often the value of good-in-hand over the still-unattainable "perfect" cannot be overstated. Speed over perfection is the idea that moving quickly with a good-enough decision is often far more valuable than delaying action in pursuit of a flawless plan.

In business and life, waiting for the perfect decision can mean missing opportunities, because timing often matters as much as quality. A good decision made swiftly keeps momentum, sparks learning, and leaves room to adjust if needed.

A perfect decision, on the other hand, might never come—or might arrive too late to be relevant. The key is knowing when the stakes demand thoroughness and when progress is more important than precision. In fast-changing environments, speed often beats perfection, because even imperfect action creates feedback, clarity, and opportunity that standing still doesn't offer. Failing quickly means learning quickly.

However, when it came to naming our fledgling company, one teammate wouldn't let us settle until we had a better name. I fought this briefly over my desire to check things off "the list," but he reminded me in his wisdom that we needed to ruminate on it for a few days. The name needed to be worthy of our endeavor. The world had come to a standstill, and a few extra days wouldn't change our trajectory.

His words resonated with me and still do to this day. Sometimes we have to stop, take a breath, and live with something. Time, while finite, is not always meant to be lived at breakneck speed.

So, we ruminated. We breathed. We sat in silence. And JoinIn was born.

BUILDING THE PLANE AND FLYING IT AT THE SAME TIME

Each of us adapted fast, took on new roles, and leaned into unfamiliar challenges. It was, without a doubt, the most unified our company had ever been. That unity turned into momentum. Our collaboration placed us in a position to be seen as leading the way as experts in this new virtual event-space world.

For two months we worked in an inspired, collaborative, and cooperative way, bouncing ideas off each other, and allowing for experimentation and fast failure. I was back in my groove, doing what I do best. And so was my team.

Being in the south has its advantages and disadvantages in every which way you can name. What that meant for us during the pandemic was that the state of Tennessee opened back up for business in early June. We stayed true to the guidelines put forth by local government officials but welcomed everyone back to the office, if they felt comfortable returning.

My team returned to the office supercharged with an all-for-one mentality. We continued what we'd started over Zoom in March and April. JoinIn was on the verge of readiness for a public launch, and as a team we were finding new ways to succeed.

It was wonderful.

JoinIn went live to the world July 1, 2020, less than six months after that February phone call.

My core team demonstrated flexibility, adaptability, and resilience. They learned everything they could about streaming and moved from producing live shows to TV broadcasts overnight. We partnered with a great vendor who built us a makeshift studio, and before we knew it, we were a go-to solution for virtual events.

There were so many people who contributed, and as much as I lament what was to come, I could not have been prouder of the contributions of every member of our team.

What made it so great? It was a rare time of completely unselfish, collaborative teamwork with no personal agendas.

More importantly, for me as a leader, it was a period when I dropped the need to be liked by everyone. A time of crisis cuts out all of the bullshit. We were suddenly in startup mode and we made decisions based on survival as our primary objective. Nothing else mattered. I didn't have the space to try to please everyone. The mission was paramount. There was no room for like-me culture. I'll have more to say on that shortly.

ACTION: BE THE 14 PERCENT

COVID was pretty special, but as you've seen, we're bound to face another disruption soon enough. Disruptions like these can set you up for a huge leap or relegate you to the back of the pack. Disruptions can occur in both your business and personal life.

While the 14 percent was uniquely tied to businesses that reinvest in themselves, I like to tie the 14 percent to an exclusive club of individuals who chose a different path across their life as a whole. They pause long enough to reinvest in what's real—their mindset, their habits, their purpose—and then build outward from there.

Whether the disruption is global or deeply personal, the starting point is the same: authenticity before activity, intention before motion.

You are the ones who rise, rebuild, and redefine what's possible—by first refusing to perform and instead choosing to grow toward a No Zero Days mindset.

REINVEST IN THE ONE THING YOU CAN CONTROL

When disruption hits, the easiest thing to neglect is yourself. In fact, if the worst possible thing happened to me tomorrow, I would close my laptop, grab my AirPods and a bottle of water, and go work out and invest in myself first. Only after that would my mind be clear enough to think about how to navigate the situation at hand.

The 14 percent don't start with external factors; rather, they take inventory. They cast their gaze inward and ask: *What can I strengthen right now? What can I control right now?* Start there.

> ## REFLECTION
>
> Write down one area where you've been coasting—mentally, physically, or relationally—and what a small, daily reinvestment of energy in that area could look like.

CHAPTER FIVE

THE QUIET DRIFT

Even though JoinIn was flourishing by every metric, the war within some days was almost too much to bear, even with the validation and success we were seeing.

I'd get up from my desk, knock on the door of a team member who knew all that was going on, and say, "I know it's only eleven in the morning, but I have nothing left in the tank, and I'm going to scream if I don't get out of here." And then I'd leave the office.

The pain was real. The whisper was screaming at me. And while we were building cool stuff, I felt like I was burning from the inside out.

No matter who you are—a stay-at-home mom, a first-time founder, a business leader, or someone working a steady 9-to-5—the numbness can creep in. That quiet drift—subtle, slow, and almost imperceptible—pulls you away from clarity and purpose.

It's not burnout.

It's not failure.

It's the slow fade of meaning when progress no longer feels personal. The next raise, the next zero added to the bottom line, the next achievement on the family checklist—none of it seems to move the needle inside you.

You might remember the spark that drove you to take a risk, or the idea that kept you up at night. Maybe you're still chasing it. Or maybe you've arrived—by all external standards—and yet something still feels off. You built the thing. You checked the boxes.

- ☐ House in the right neighborhood. Check.
- ☐ Car from the right manufacturer. Check.
- ☐ Kids in the right school. Check.

But that lingering question remains: *Is this it?*

This chapter is about when success stops feeling real and the voice that once pushed you forward becomes difficult for you to hear. It's like boiling to death one degree at a time: it happens so slowly you don't realize you're dying until it's too late.

But you are. And it starts with the quiet drift.

THE HAMSTER WHEEL

Workaholism. We all hate this word, and we certainly don't want to admit that we've fallen into its trap. We don't become workaholics overnight. We start with pure intentions. We believe that if we work harder than everyone else, we will be successful. Better yet, we'll be loved, liked, accepted, content, and happy. If we work harder, satisfaction will come.

Work first becomes our escape, and then it becomes our drug of choice. It becomes the thing we hide behind to avoid difficult situations or acknowledge our own lack of peace.

You might be thinking, *That's not me,* but if you say things to yourself like, "I can't make time for that school event," or "I need to cancel dinner tonight with a long-time friend" so you can work, and you justify your decision to work more because *you're* the one providing, you might be exhibiting some symptoms of this addiction.

Soon you'll have trained everyone you care about that you're not available. You're working.

The phone will stop ringing and the invitations will stop coming. Others will quietly quit asking you to participate in their lives. Your relationships drift into shallower waters.

The work-work-work mindset slowly erodes our soul and our inner identity. We no longer identify as who we are.

> **WE BECOME WHAT WE DO. AND WE'RE DESPERATE FOR RECOGNITION, FOR OUR ACHIEVEMENTS TO MATTER. WE WANT TO PLEASE EVERYONE. AND SO, WHAT WE DO IS WHAT WE THINK OTHERS WANT US TO DO.**

We become a chameleon, even to those closest to us. Without realizing it, we ask ourselves: *Who do I need to be at home? Who do I need to be at work? Who do I need to be to my friends?* … And once we figure it out, we play the role we believe we need to play.

We wear so many masks we're not even sure what lies at our core.

There's no room for authenticity when we're pleasing everyone but ourselves. But we can't stop running because we're on that hamster wheel, chasing the success we've promised everyone around us we were going to go get.

And so, without the anchor of our three pillars and No Zero Days, we live in performance mode, working harder, working more—not realizing how far we are drifting from our core self.

ACTION: THE DRIFT DETECTOR

You hit the goals. You built the thing. You made it out of the grind and into the life you thought you wanted. And yet still it comes. That quiet, deflating whisper: *Is this it?*

If you've ever found yourself asking that—especially at the moment you were supposed to feel the most fulfilled—you're not broken. You're just paying attention.

And now it's time to face the version of you that's been running at full speed, hoping momentum would drown out the silence. You've mastered the art of performance but feel like a stranger at home. You've been trading joy for validation. Purpose for permission. Presence for production.

If you've been willing to live with the discomfort of the question, *you may finally be ready to hear the truth behind it.*

Is this it?

Your challenge is to disrupt that drift. To interrupt the numbness. And to ask the uncomfortable questions you've likely been avoiding. This challenge is about waking yourself up.

STEP 1: NAME THE DRIFT

Start by getting honest about the signs that something feels off.

You might still be achieving, still showing up, still performing, but inside, the spark has faded.

Drift doesn't always look like burnout; sometimes it looks like busyness without meaning.

> ## *REFLECTION*
> Write down three ways drift shows up for you—maybe it's restlessness, numbness, or the sense that success doesn't feel like success anymore. Naming it is how you begin to take away its power.

STEP 2: SPOT YOUR HAMSTER WHEEL

What patterns keep you running but not moving?

Overworking, saying "yes" when you mean "no," chasing validation, or measuring worth by output—these are signs of performance without meaning. Make a list of how this shows up in your life.

Ask yourself: *What am I avoiding by staying this busy?*

Get real with yourself. It's okay if it's an ugly truth. The only person you have to acknowledge that truth to right now is you.

STEP 3: BUILD YOUR DRIFT DETECTOR

Drift starts as a whisper and, if you let it, builds up to a deafening scream. Build your early-warning system so you can hear it before it takes over.

List three personal signals that tell you you're slipping into the quiet drift of workaholism: canceling plans, ignoring your healthy habits, or feeling detached from people you love.

Next to each signal, write one counter-action you'll take when it appears.

If you find yourself withdrawing, reach out.

If you're overworking, step away and reset.

If you've lost focus on what matters, revisit your pillars and realign.

Why It Matters

You can beat the drift with awareness, consistency, and forward motion. Every time you take a single, meaningful step—every day you end that counts as a No Zero Day—you prove to yourself that the current doesn't control you; you're the one in charge.

STEP 4: RECONNECT WITH MEANING

Realigning yourself once after encountering the drift doesn't mean you've beaten it forever. You'll encounter it again.

Which of your three pillars do you feel most out of alignment with right now? Choose to take one action today that moves you toward it.

Even the smallest move—a text, a pause, a walk, a thank-you—counts, as long as it's in service of one of your pillars. A *No Zero Day* is about doing something that *matters*.

CHAPTER SIX

THE POINT OF NO RETURN

In real life—and on the road to building a No Zero Days mindset—there are moments that mark fundamental shifts. Sometimes it's a painful personal decision, like ending a relationship that no longer serves your growth. Other times, it's a bold business move: restructuring your company, walking away from misaligned work, or finally saying "no" to revenue that costs your peace.

The point of no return is rarely clean. It's messy, emotional, and often strips away the version of yourself you once recognized. That's why you're here—reading this book—not because everything makes sense and feels great, but because something inside you is stirring, wanting more. Maybe you feel a shift. Or maybe you feel nothing at all, and that numbness is its own kind of signal.

Crossing this threshold means choosing growth even when it feels like loss. For me, it was surrendering to the tidal wave of everything I had buried: unmet expectations, unspoken truths, and choices meant to please "them" but that never quite pleased me.

THE INVISIBLE WEIGHT

I flew in from London in October and, as I often did, took the long way home from the airport, detouring on the back roads.

As I drove, I noticed the rusting colors of the changing leaves and overcast skies. They matched my solemn heart. Fall was normally a happy time for me, but over the last several years I'd only felt numb.

That day, I couldn't breathe. I turned onto Highway 96 and saw a gentle fog had settled into the valley, but then the Natchez Trace Bridge came into view, and for a moment the pressure on my chest eased up.

It was often a place where I could find respite. I drove up to the bridge and, like I had so many times before, parked and got out and walked across, the occasional car passing below. From the top I made a phone call to one of my long-time friends.

As soon as he answered I blurted out, "I don't know how much longer I can do this."

No, I wasn't suicidal. I wasn't going to jump. But the weight on my soul was so heavy. I didn't know how much longer I could resent having to go home. The internal conflict was mounting.

No matter how much I achieved, it was never enough to make my wife happy. She felt that I always put work first. I didn't know how to make her understand I was working so much because that was how I knew how to provide. That was how I showed love. I can see now that I was approaching the lower levels of development in my Type 3 personality. My greatest strength, my ability to produce, which I thought would save me, instead served to form the chasm in my marriage.

I thought the hours I was putting in demonstrated my love and commitment to my family. But to my wife, those long hours I put in at the office didn't feel like love. My behavior felt like abandonment.

It took me a long time to see this. At first her resentment of me felt like she couldn't see what I was providing; it felt like a deep rejection of who I was and not like a plea for connection. It felt like she was ungrateful for all of my hard work.

I could have left it there and pointed the blame for my failing marriage at my wife or at the problems of the world that forced me to work so much. But I had to learn to look in the mirror and do the hard personal work myself. I have spent time in deep examination and I can now see life through both sets of lenses.

I adored my kids. However, I know I was a terrible father to them at the time. I was only existing at home, and I wanted more than just existing, chasing, and climbing with no end in sight.

Our home was out on the west side of Franklin in a planned community. It was "the" place to live. By most measures, I had arrived. It had more than 5,000 square feet of space spread over three levels and was the only one like it in our neighborhood.

The kryptonite of the design was that we could separate from each other anytime we wanted, and that is what my wife and I did.

Is this what I've worked for? Is this what my sacrifices have brought? To live together like ghosts in a heartless house?

Is this it?

I'd entered my early forties and begun to really question what my true purpose was. This is where you might expect to hear something like, "I wanted to be a father more than anything else."

The truth is, I saw fatherhood as something I was failing at.

More than anything, I wanted the approval of those I respected, admired, and loved. And I only knew one way to get it.

I had given up on being the husband my wife wanted. My marriage felt like a lost cause; but *if* I could create financial freedom for my family, *then* I could be the father my girls wanted and at least be successful in that role.

I chose more work instead of more connection. And in the months that followed, the drift only widened.

That admission on the bridge changed me. Simply vocalizing where I was made it possible for me to hear the whisper, gave credence to the invisible weight, and allowed me to look at what opportunities were in front of me.

I was finally acknowledging *my* desires without everyone else's filter.

I hung up the phone, took several deep breaths, and panned the fall trees with a 360-degree spin.

I didn't know what this change meant, but I knew that the status quo was no longer an option. The whisper was clearly audible. I slowly walked back to my car, slid in behind the wheel, and, feeling somewhat galvanized, drove home. I missed my girls. They were getting caught in our crossfire.

At the very least I could walk in the door, hug them, and share my surprises from London with them. They offered unconditional love, and I would lean into that and return it as best I could as I figured out what that moment atop the bridge meant for the days ahead.

Our workaholism blinds us to the subtle shifts in life and, before we know it, we don't recognize ourselves. That life we so desperately worked to create? We're not sure it's even worth it. We got here one day at a time, one choice at a time. We may look successful on the outside, but on the inside? We're lost.

If you're feeling like you're on that same relentless hamster wheel that never delivers satisfaction no matter how fast you run, how hard you work, or how much you hustle, take the time to work through the following exercise. You are not doomed to be stuck in this hollow life.

There comes a time when looking back is no longer an option—when staying the same costs more than evolving. For high achievers like us, this moment comes in the quiet: in the middle of a fight you didn't want to have, on a bridge you didn't plan to cross, or in a decision that ends a chapter you thought would never close.

It's time to get real with yourself.

THE UNTOLD STORY

Is this it?

The question had been haunting me for months. If I had achieved everything everyone said I should, why wasn't I happier? Why wasn't I content or satisfied? I had all the trappings of success. Why did I always feel less than, hollow, and like I *still* hadn't arrived?

Those three words often rose to the surface in the quiet darkness of my home and with my partner. Yes, we tried therapy and spent a lot of time in it. Here's the thing. It can be easy to get through the top layers of therapy, but for true, life-changing progress, you have to go deep.

I can say with certainty that there were layers that I didn't explore until after our divorce was finalized. Would that exploration have saved our relationship? I don't know.

One evening I finally felt complete clarity, though it also brought heaviness. What started as a "How was your day?" conversation turned into yet another one of our toxic blowups.

I went to bed that night and thought, *If we can't come together in the darkest moment, will we ever be able to?*

The answer was no.

It felt like I'd stumbled to the bathroom in the middle of the night and fumbled for the light only to find the switch was gone. Just gone. There was no way to turn on the light. That was it.

The light switch in my marriage was gone and I wanted a divorce. I'd hit the point of no return.

* * *

It would be another month before I moved out, but I knew that it was over. That moment of clarity I'd experienced on the Natchez Trace Bridge was finally resolved.

I never took the decision to file for divorce lightly. We'd spent nearly twenty years together. It's heartbreaking enough to feel the pain in your own heart and see it mirrored in your spouse's eyes.

But when your daughter says, "Daddy, I don't see you and Mommy ever kiss," or, "Daddy, why do you always seem sad?"—and you realize the pain you thought was private has spilled into their world—it knocks the wind out of you.

I asked myself, *What do I want my kids to say later in life when they're asked if their parents are still married?* Given my present circumstances, I could only see two viable options.

- *Yeah, they're married. I mean they stayed together but they don't really like each other, and I didn't really see a loving relationship at home.*

- *No, my parents got divorced when I was a kid, but they both found happiness the second time around and now it's like I have two great families.*

For me the answer was clear. I asked for a divorce and started the process of ending our marriage.

Maybe I won't get married again. However, if I do, it will be a full-circle moment that will give my daughters the example they deserve. In the years since my divorce, I've done a lot of personal healing. I can say with confidence that I know what love really is and what it means to give love and receive it.

It's much more than just "not fighting."

If it's not in the cards for me to find a lifelong partner, I know this much: I can be the present father my girls deserve—and model the kind of partner I hope they choose someday. They come first in my life, along with my faith. I know that with No Zero Days as my filter, I will make choices that support my pillars first and foremost, and because I am gifted at achieving what I set out to do, I will be present and engaged with my family and my faith.

SHOULD YOU STAY OR SHOULD YOU GO?

Maybe you find yourself in a similar situation: Your personal relationships are strained. Maybe it's a decision you're facing about whether or not to abandon a company you've been with for a long time, and it will be a big shakeup.

Whatever your dilemma, if you're facing one, take heart in knowing you are not alone by any means. I can't say whether a new organization or a divorce is the right or wrong choice for you. Honestly, no one should. Only you can know your truth and what you can live with. Only you live in your shoes.

The words of my therapist ring true here. Whatever decision you make, be sure that you understand this key thought process.

Walk down the middle of the road and keep your gaze straight ahead. In one direction you stay together; in the other you leave. Regardless of which direction you choose, the following will be true.

On one side, people will say, "You're doing the right thing."

On the other, people will say, "You're an evil person," and, "What's wrong with you? Shame!"

No matter what you choose—stay or go—these two groups of people will exist.

So, make the decision you can live with and recognize you might wake up one day with regret.

If you can look ahead and accept that reality, then you free yourself to make the decision that is best for you. Once I was able to accept that there was no way to please everyone and knew that I was going to have to live with whatever came after it, my decision became clear.

I'd hit the point of no return—and some might say a sad one. But without it I would never have gotten to a No Zero Days mentality.

ACTION: RECOGNIZE YOUR POINT OF NO RETURN

Your challenge is to examine your own version of the switch going missing: that moment when the old way stopped being possible.

STEP 1: NAME THE MOMENT YOU KNEW

What is your bridge moment?

I could have made that day on the Natchez Trace Bridge about endings, but instead I learned it was about being able to breathe again.

It was when that quiet voice inside me declared: *I can't keep living this way.*

Think of your own bridge moment—when something in you said, *No more pretending.* Capture the instant you realized something had to change.

Describe it in one sentence.

> ## *REFLECTION*
>
> *"The moment I knew I couldn't go back was ..."*
>
> Write that sentence down, and as you do, note in the margins—or underneath—what emotions surfaced? Was it relief, fear, guilt, peace? If you can, seek to identify the context behind that emotion.

STEP 2: IDENTIFY WHAT YOU WERE PROTECTING

List what you were preserving by stepping forward—your peace, future, children, your truth.

These were your non-negotiable reasons for living. Check to see if they correlate with your three pillars.

STEP 3: HEAD OFF THE NEXT INEVITABILITY

Consider where you resent spending time or energy in your life. What do you dread doing and with whom? What drives you to place your time and energy there? Is it worth it? If you stay there, will it lead to the point of no return?

Why It Matters

Growth can't happen while you're defending the person you've outgrown. When you continue to spend your most precious resource—time—on things that aren't in support of your core identity, you aren't making the space in your life for those things that are important.

STEP 4: BUILD THE NEW FOUNDATION

Remind yourself what you're making space for by listing your three non-negotiable pillars.

Plan to take at least one action this week that honors each of them.

* * *

The point of no return is a threshold, and it doesn't have to mean an ending. Crossing it requires discomfort, taking ownership without deflection, and learning what really matters for your next chapter.

You don't need to know what that chapter looks like. But if you aren't truly honest with yourself, you'll likely just repeat the chapter you just finished.

No Zero Days begins here, if you show up with courage. And if I can do it, I believe you can, too.

PART THREE

THE HARD WAY DOWN

If there is one thing I want you to take away from this book (in addition to a No Zero Days mentality), it would be this next realization.

While I'd found some relief in the decision to end my marriage, one big key fact escaped me: At some point your inner worlds will collide and there will be a reckoning.

In my effort to ignore the pain and not deal with myself or what I'd been through, I poured myself into the thing that fed my broken soul, or so I thought.

I got back to work. Things with the company were clicking and each roar of victory allowed me to ignore the gentle nudges I was receiving from quieter voices of wisdom.

After all, they didn't know what I was going through. They hadn't founded a brand new and very successful company during the pandemic all while going through a divorce. They had no idea what I was capable of.

My marriage had already paid one price. I couldn't let my company do the same. Little did I know at the time:

> ## COMPARTMENTALIZATION WORKS UNTIL IT DOESN'T.

I thought I could keep the destruction of my personal life from bleeding into my work life.

Arrogant, right? I can see that now.

We Achievers don't like to slow down, rest, or recover. We like to think the work will save us. But something like the death of a marriage you've worked long and hard at calls for a pause.

What I should have done is listened to the voices that said, *Stop. Just for a moment. Gather yourself. Recover. Rediscover.*

I needed someone I trusted to walk into my office, sit me down, and say, *Let's not worry about all of the bad choices you've made already, because that induces shame. We'll get to those later.*

But just for today, STOP.

Stop casting a vision when you can't see clearly. You are in no position to cast vision. You need to heal. You need to pause.

You need to invest in yourself. Don't worry. The business isn't going anywhere. We can structure it to hold the line until you're whole again. You take all the time you need to recover and find yourself.

Then, when you're ready, we'll go.

Had just such a person come into my life at the right moment, my story could have had a completely different outcome—or, at the very least, it might have been significantly less painful, costly, and messy.

If you are on the heels of emotional trauma like I was and you also are missing that mentor, please let me be that voice for you.

STOP. Pause. Recalibrate. Recenter. Find your pillars. Live with No Zero Days.

Then—and only then—step back into leadership.

Our tendencies as Achievers can bring destructive results when we are in this state. We're reactive and churning, doing just to do. We too easily trust that our past wins predict only future success, and we attempt to lead in a vacuum.

All the while we tell ourselves, *I'm great. Everything's fine. It will all work out.*

Yikes.

The stories I share with you in this section aren't pretty. But they're here to serve as a cautionary tale. Take them as further evidence that without the No Zero Days mentality that puts your experiences in alignment with your authentic self, things definitely can (and probably will) get worse before they get better.

The signs of deep dissatisfaction are subtle at first. You miss a sign here, dismiss a gut feeling there. You tell yourself, *It's just a phase; that momentum will return; I've survived worse. It's nothing worth paying attention to.*

In this section I'm sharing the shadow side of my life, the part I normally would shield from all outside eyes, and I'm doing so in the hopes that I can help *you* in some small way. I want your journey to be easier than mine was.

CHAPTER SEVEN

FRACTURES SHOW

Outwardly, things looked fine. Great, even. We were winning awards, closing projects, and celebrating milestones. But inside, I was fragmenting. Part of me still showed up strong, decisive, and driven.

At the same time, what had started as an amicable divorce became a nightmare of attorneys. I had underestimated the emotional toll, naively believing I could compartmentalize the chaos at home from the business at hand.

The other part—the quieter part—was unraveling. Questioning everything. Avoiding the mirror. My marriage had cracked. I had to be a superstar somewhere … *right?*

I did what many leaders do when doubt creeps in: I buried it beneath performance. I believed I could outwork failure, outpace mistakes, and outsmart broken systems.

That belief—rooted in ego, fed by my soul-level exhaustion— looked like confidence. That's what I projected, or tried to, as I guided the wheel, driving our company.

But I was driving blind.

TICK-TOCK, DON'T STOP

When you've clawed your way out of the dark, when the wins start stacking, and the applause grows louder, that's when arrogance finds its voice, though it masks itself as *momentum* and convinces you the rules no longer apply.

You tell yourself, *I've made it.* You believe that your past successes are proof of mastery, and you barrel forward, unchecked.

Invincibility is seductive, but it's an illusion. It's never been real. We are all breakable. The space between success and collapse is razor-thin—and it only takes a handful of missteps to fall through it.

Every great dynasty eventually falls—not from a lack of power, but from a loss of perspective. Those who rise again are the ones who remain vigilant, grounded, and aware of the subtle shifts within themselves.

Unchecked success creates distance—from your team, your values, and your own internal compass. You stop listening, stop reflecting, and start reacting. When that happens, you make decisions from ego, not clarity.

That's what makes the arrogance of winning so treacherous—it disguises itself as confidence, but operates like blindness.

What I failed to realize in those moments—what I now see clearly—is that the only antidote to this misalignment is intention and the daily discipline of No Zero Days.

To this day, I'm still navigating the ripple effects of that season—not just the decisions I made, but the ones I didn't. Chief among them: I didn't stop. I didn't pull any chips off the table. I kept going full tilt, believing that was strength and that slowing down meant failure.

But here's the truth: Sometimes, taking chips off the table *is* the strategy. Taking a pause doesn't mean giving up. Six months is a blink in the lifespan of a healthy business. I know now that slowing down doesn't kill momentum; it gives you the power to sustain it.

Some of you reading this might move too slowly. You overthink, delay, and hesitate.

Others—like me—move too fast. We ignore the warning signs and barrel ahead, calling it courage.

The truth lies somewhere in between. There's wisdom in the fable of the tortoise and the hare—but the real trick is knowing when to sprint and when to pause. Not everything has to happen *now*. At times it's necessary to stop, clear your head, and recalibrate. The race is long. And it's not won in a single heat. This is about sustainability.

High performers don't burn out because they can't win—they burn out because they won't stop.

Sometimes your best move is to sit in the quiet and finally listen.

BLURRY VISION

I've told you about the mentor I needed and didn't have (or didn't listen to). Let me tell you what I had instead: people encouraging me to pour gas on the fire. To go full force. Climb the next summit.

And that's where my overconfidence and pride took root. It whispered, *You've done this before, you'll do it again, no problem. Just do what you've always done before. Keep working, keep going, keep doing. You can't help but succeed. Everything you want is just around the corner.*

I needed to lead, but I only had blurry vision. As leaders, we're supposed to inspire. We provide the *what* and the *why* and we let our team figure out the *how*.

If you have the right team with the right skills and attitude, they'll rally to the picture of the future you paint. They'll astonish you with the lengths they'll go to support your vision … unless you cast a blurry vision and they don't understand what you're doing or why.

As my marriage was in its death throes, I had no vision to cast. Most days I couldn't even tell you why I was in the office. If you'd asked me what was next, I'd have said, "We're going to make more money."

Is making more money a bad thing? No, of course not. But money on its own isn't a vision for the future. Your team needs to know *what* "more" means and *why* they should create it.

How could I inspire my team with visions of an extraordinary future if I couldn't even articulate it for myself?

ACTION: COST-BENEFIT DECISION ANALYSIS

Are you going for fool's gold? Or are your dreams worth the pursuit?

Do your standard cost-benefit analysis on the win you're currently pursuing—or the success you're chasing. Consider how that pursuit affects the personal, spiritual, and business facets of your life. "More money" might not have the return you expect.

Once your pillars are in place, the results of your analysis become even easier to ascertain. Does what you're chasing support them? It's your life, and with a No Zero Days mentality you will make the choices that serve you best. Start with these action items as you examine what you are chasing.

STEP 1: PAUSE THE PERFORMANCE LOOP

Ask: *Am I leading from clarity or exhaustion?*

> ### REFLECTION
>
> Write one major decision and the emotion driving it.
> Is this decision coming from pressure or alignment?

STEP 2: REVISIT THE COST TO "KEEP GOING"

List three ways that your pace costs you.

Add one benefit that could come from slowing down.

STEP 3: DEFINE WINNING

Take five minutes to define success beyond money or applause.

Write what "enough" means to you.

Hint: It should correlate with your pillars.

Why It Matters

If you never define what "enough" is, you'll never know when to stop.

STEP 4: DECIDE FROM WHOLENESS, NOT WOUNDEDNESS

Before you make your next big move, ask yourself:

Have I healed from the last big upset?

Am I seeing the whole picture or just the pain?

Will future me thank present me for this choice?

WHO NEEDS BUY-IN?

Our company was doing well. We'd survived and even thrived during the pandemic era.

I spoke freely about growth and what I wanted to do but didn't stop to consider how blurry my message was or how that lack of precision would affect our team. Worse, I never sought their buy-in.

THE INVESTMENT THAT TAUGHT ME EVERYTHING

I had crossed my point of no return in filing for divorce and was ready to move on to bigger and better things in my world view.

Amidst all that was going on, I chose to sell the office building I'd purchased nearly four years earlier. We put it on the market and it sold in three weeks.

In my mind, this was perfect. We were going to move up to a better space. A company growing at the pace we were should certainly have a fancy new office space, and why not? We were flying high. Winning contracts. We deserved it.

How many times have you had a decision in front of you that seems perfect and yet is fast moving? If you're like me, your thoughts follow this chain:

This is perfect.

If I don't move quickly, we'll miss it.

This must be meant for me.

That uneasiness I'm feeling is nothing. I'm only feeling it because it's moving fast. I can do this.

Sound familiar? I'd often followed a "ready, fire, aim" mindset over the course of my career. This was no different.

When I was challenged about my decision making, I knew how to give the right answers. I could deliver a master class in anticipating questions and providing the pacifying answer, then selling that answer until no one asked me again.

Besides, I had the profit alchemy. Everything I touched seemed to turn to gold. Inside me, a sense of invincibility was building. Without irony, I held the unshakeable belief that if we needed more money, we would just go get it.

The invincibility I felt was at war with sound decision making. I was convinced I was thinking clearly, that I was incapable of being wrong.

I did have a vision, but I hoarded it. Maybe I didn't want to be challenged; I wanted to be lauded. I wanted to pull everything off and present it on a platter to my team.

My idea was to build the best culture center in Tennessee. Our new office was going to be the epicenter for a nationwide expansion. We'd have offices in Las Vegas and New York City over the next five years.

I talked myself into the new space without consulting my team. I ignored the voices in my head telling me to slow down.

I signed the lease agreement during the heart of the pandemic when everyone else was fleeing their offices. I got the office at an unheard-of rate and secured a significant tenant improvement budget with no cost increase to my lease.

What I really wanted was to land that elusive feeling: "This is it!"

No matter how much success I celebrated during the day, I went home empty. No matter how many times I said "This is it!" in the quiet dark of an empty house, the whisper inside me would come again, asking, *Is this it?*

But with this lease, I knew I was a deal maker. I felt like a hero. I remember coming home that night and thinking, *This will be one of my moments.*

I don't do anything halfway. I poured over the new office space design. I touched everything from the countertops to the carpet insets to the plant wall to custom furniture and posh art. It was going to be a place our people called home, where they felt creative and free to do their best work.

What I failed to acknowledge, especially to myself, was that underneath my stated dreams, I was investing in the environment *because it made me feel important and satisfied my ego.* Our business would have been just fine had we never sold the original office building. If I'm being honest, this was all for me, not my team.

REALITY INTRUDES

Following the sale of our building, we moved our team into a temporary office while construction began on our new buildout. If I trace the timeline of lessons I had to learn the hard way, they begin here.

I've always seen myself as an agent of change. Change is creative fuel. Whether it's swapping out a room's design, changing a strategy midstream, or—in this case—moving offices, the shift gives me life.

But what gives a founder energy doesn't always do the same for our teams.

What I failed to see was this: My team wasn't ready for a move like the one I'd initiated. We'd just emerged from the haze of COVID and were exhausted and weary.

We'd had a few small wins and were just regaining some footing, and then I pulled the rug out from under them. Our office sold before the buildout for the new space was complete.

We moved from a vibrant, familiar workspace into a cold, unfinished shell with dirty carpet, scattered desks, and the kind of chaos that drains energy rather than inspires it.

Every human experiences change differently. I don't think I was wrong for moving fast. I was just blind to how unprepared my team was for the pace. I made the mistake of assuming everyone could see what I saw. I believed they trusted the destination, even if the path was unclear.

But vision doesn't scale without translation. I didn't pause long enough to sit with each department, to ask what they needed, or to explain where we were headed. I just moved. Because that's what I've always done.

Speed isn't a strategy if no one's moving with you.

This is where the cracks in our once-invincible team began. Without me achieving their buy-in on decisions, my team felt like they were losing their compass. At first, they were hairline fractures—missed meetings, later arrivals, early exits, minor frictions between teams.

The signs were subtle but real. And I missed them. Partly because I was looking the other way. But mostly because I was still fighting a war within.

I've heard it said that you don't realize the stress you're carrying in a crisis until the crisis ends. That's true. We humans are remarkably resilient. We normalize dysfunction just to survive. We keep moving because slowing down feels like drowning. But what I didn't see then—what I now understand—is that I was showing up every day with blurry vision and fractured energy. My ability to lead was compromised. And the people around me could feel it.

ACTION: ESCAPE THE URGENCY TRAP

There's a moment in every leader's life where momentum feels like a drug. After crossing the point of no return, you likely find yourself doubling down, sprinting harder, chasing more. The energy is high. The results are impressive. But is it real?

This challenge is designed to help you recognize when your performance is a mask and your *pace* is something else you're hiding behind. Sometimes the hardest thing for a high performer to do is stop.

STEP 1: CHECK THE MIRROR BEFORE YOU MOVE

Urgency often disguises insecurity. The faster you move, the less you see what's really driving you. Before you make your next big decision, pause long enough to ask: *Am I leading from clarity or from a desire for validation?*

Before you sign, send, or say yes to something urgent—ask one simple question: *Does this decision strengthen our shared vision or does it just satisfy my need for motion?*

> ### REFLECTION
> When was the last time you made a big move in order to feel significant or important instead of aligned? What would it look like to lead from security instead of ego?

STEP 2: BUILD CONFIDENCE THROUGH COLLABORATION

Your team—and your family—don't need a perfect leader. They need an *honest one.* Invite them into the process, even if your vision feels fragile.

When you share early, you give others permission to care. When you hoard your ideas, you only protect your ego.

Pick one upcoming decision and bring two trusted voices into the conversation before you make the final call. Listen actively to their perspective, but realize you don't need their permission to proceed. If you're living No Zero Days, you'll know you have the right choice when the decision aligns with your pillars.

STEP 3: TRANSLATE VISION INTO OWNERSHIP

Buy-in happens through shared understanding.

If your vision can't be repeated by your team in their own words, it's not clear enough, and you probably don't have buy-in.

The next time you share something that you know it's important to achieve understanding on, ask the recipient of your vision to repeat it for you in their own words.

WHY IT MATTERS

People don't rally behind what they're told. They rally behind what they helped shape. Clarity and confirmed understanding create confidence and buy-in—for you and everyone following you.

STEP 4: LEAD THE LONG GAME

Urgency wins headlines; alignment builds legacies. When the next "perfect" opportunity shows up, don't chase it alone—lead with intention.

When things feel urgent, gather your people, name the fears, outline the stakes, and move deliberately forward together. Simple to say, but not easy to execute—unless you are in alignment with your pillars.

CHAPTER EIGHT

FAILING SLOW

A THREE-DAY PIVOT

There was a three-day stretch in September 2021 when it felt like everything turned. All the doubt, the turmoil, the internal questioning—it seemed as if it were finally behind me. On the surface, it looked like I was emerging from a pitch-black tunnel into a blinding light of success.

Three days in a row:

- **Day One:** We delivered a global event for the world's second-largest social media company. Check.

- **Day Two:** My divorce mediation finalized. Check.

- **Day Three:** I got the call—we won a multimillion-dollar proposal. Check.

I couldn't have scripted a cleaner ending to one chapter or a more triumphant beginning to the next. The momentum was intoxicating. I felt untouchable. I felt I'd made it.

Emphasis on *"I."*

Somewhere between survival mode and scaling mode, I had abandoned the empathy, clarity, and awareness that defined our rebound during the first months of the pandemic.

My team? They were mentally and emotionally drained. And I kept pushing the throttle forward, asking for more and more from them, without checking the gauges.

What started as a three-day pivot could have been the beginning of our company's next chapter. Instead, it was the start of our unraveling.

We didn't have contracts in hand yet, but I began making moves as if we did—setting strategy, shifting operations, and building around a future that wasn't yet real. It was the classic mistake: counting chickens before they hatch.

In my rush to capitalize on the moment, I slipped into directive mode—barking strategy without inviting collaboration. I'd forgotten one of the most important principles that had always guided me: **fail fast.**

The "fail fast" mindset is about experimenting: You move quickly, find the faults early, and pivot toward what works and away from what doesn't before too much time, money, or energy is wasted.

> **FAILING FAST IS ALL ABOUT RECOGNIZING WHEN IT'S TIME TO WALK AWAY— NOT DOUBLING DOWN JUST BECAUSE YOU'VE ALREADY INVESTED.**

Failing fast lets you experiment without worrying about being wrong, because you'll adapt quickly. Failing fast doesn't let you stay with your mistakes. It's designed to allow you to be nimble, agile, and responsive.

I violated that mindset in every direction.

On one hand, JoinIn had been very successful during the pandemic. On the other, we were struggling to adapt it to life after the pandemic. I held on and continued to invest money and resources into the product, instead of seeing it for what it was: a successful stopgap that had run its course. After everything we'd invested, surely just a little more would make it work. Or so I told myself.

A startup venture I attempted in an entirely new industry? It was dead long before we finally pulled the plug, yet I kept investing in hopes of justifying the idea—because I couldn't possibly be *wrong*, right?

Fail fast. Your gut is often right, and you see when things aren't working. Adjust with intention or pull the plug and move on.

I DESERVE THIS

By the end of the year, I was spent. Not tired—*depleted*. The kind of exhaustion that doesn't go away with a few good nights of sleep. I convinced myself I needed a change of scenery. I had earned it. I deserved time away. *Of course I did. Hadn't I just been through major stress?*

So, I flew to California and checked into the Montage Hotel in Laguna Beach. It was supposed to be a one-week reset. Instead, I stayed for nearly three weeks. When the final bill came, I blinked for a moment, then dropped my card on the counter with confidence. *I deserve this*, I told myself. *I'm going to live a little.*

That phrase "I deserve this" became my mantra heading into the next year.

And on the surface, it made sense. I had just made it through a global pandemic. I had finalized a divorce. I had led a team through the fog of uncertainty and somehow come out the other side. My narrative was airtight: *Of course I'm entitled to blow off some steam.*

What I failed to see was how entitlement and exhaustion were quietly forming a toxic bond that I used to justify reckless financial decisions under the illusion of reward.

I doubled down on "living." I'm a lifelong college basketball fan, and I've been a Duke fan since 1986. When I heard 2022 would be Coach K's final season, I knew I had to go to the last Duke vs. UNC game at Cameron Indoor. I brought my father figure to celebrate with me. He had always paid my way when I was growing up, and it was my turn. Truthfully, it was a genuine bucket list moment.

And yet—it wasn't enough.

Three weeks later, Duke made it to the Final Four. Against UNC. A matchup that had *never* happened on that stage. I didn't hesitate. I bought center court VIP tickets—two of them—as part of a package deal. And then I went alone.

Yes, it was electric. Yes, it was unforgettable. But I couldn't fully enjoy it. I told myself I would go next year … and every year after. I watered down the experience with false promises of endless tomorrows. I was addicted to distraction disguised as reward. I was desperately trying to fill a hole in my soul with anything but faith.

What looked like celebration was actually avoidance.

Two problems were surfacing:

First, *living*, to me, had come to mean indulgence—extravagant escapes that masked the deeper disconnection from myself. I was playing with money I hadn't earned and acting like there was no tomorrow.

But I still hadn't answered that nagging question, *Is this it?* I distracted myself with the shiny veneer of each new experience to avoid that reckoning.

I found myself fully immersed in once-in-a-lifetime experiences, yet remained emotionally absent. Smiling, but numb. Accomplished, but empty. I was hiding—from others, yes—but mostly from myself.

And here's what I now know with painful clarity: You may be able to hide from others, but you can never really hide from yourself. Not if you still expect to find peace and contentment.

There will be a reckoning. You can choose a controlled burn now or wait for the full collapse later. For me, the walls were already beginning to crack with the signs of this strain.

And still, I didn't want to see it. Because acknowledging it meant facing the truth: Arrogance had blurred my self-awareness. Entitlement erased my boundaries. And my deep-seated need to be liked and to have everyone's approval was creating an identity crisis that couldn't hold.

A PLEASE-LIKE-ME CULTURE

Although we closed out the year on what looked like a high note, the reality inside our walls told a different story. Our people were exhausted.

The entire industry had endured a brutal year—paralyzed in Q1 by uncertainty, hesitant to rehire even as vaccines rolled out, and scrambling through the back half of the year to meet the pent-up demand.

We didn't staff up. We didn't build systems. And both of those missteps would come back to haunt us.

Shortly after the three-day pivot, I took a small group of core team members—those who had weathered the entirety of the pandemic with us—to lunch. I intended for it to be a listening session.

I thought I'd created a culture where people could push back on my bad ideas. I told my people, "If you disagree, come talk to me."

But words aren't enough to make people feel comfortable going to complain to the CEO.

Now that I had officially opened the door to feedback, what I got was a full-on assault.

One team member in particular let it all fly. Frustration over workload. Frustration over leadership. Frustration over culture. I sat there, absorbing the criticism. And while some of it had merit, it also revealed a deeper entitlement that I had unwittingly cultivated.

But that's not what I took away from the meeting with my staff. Nope. Instead, I walked away knowing there was someone on the team who *didn't like me*. In my unhealthy need to be liked, I focused on fixing that instead of addressing the underlying issues that were creating the cracks.

I allowed cultural cancers to grow because I couldn't stomach conflict.

I didn't course-correct misalignment; I accommodated it.

I'll share one specific example regarding an employee who had been with me for years. They were a genuinely good person, full of heart. But they weren't succeeding in the role they were hired to fill—not because they weren't trying, but because I'd failed to lead them with clarity. I allowed our history to rationalize their poor performance, and my desire to be liked led me to avoid the hard conversation that I knew would ultimately be necessary.

When we finally sat down, I waffled. I tiptoed. I knew we needed to part ways, but my desire to be liked—and to avoid conflict—won out. Against all counsel, I repositioned them in the company without providing clear direction or expectations.

The result? More confusion. Less clarity. And even greater frustration for them and the team.

Instead of pruning what needed to go, I nurtured dysfunction—believing my team would interpret it as loyalty and respond in kind. They didn't.

The bottom line? At the most critical time in our company, I'd invested in the wrong things.

I invested in people. But I'd failed to invest in leadership.

READ THAT AGAIN.

We hired some great people. They were all very qualified, but I hired them and walked away, having said the equivalent of, *Welcome! I'm glad you're here. Do your job.* I assumed that after thirty days they'd understand my DNA and my vision, and it would all magically blossom into greatness.

I trusted my team so much so that I began to chase acquisition ideas and invested heavily in another startup that wasn't even related to my core industry. I was chasing greatness in all the wrong ways and in all the wrong places.

My focus was misaligned and it played out as we signed a luxury car brand that could have redefined our agency's future.

But instead of building on that opportunity, we stumbled. Contracts were sloppy, adequate handoffs never happened, and I assumed the team would recalibrate on their own. We skipped process and let oversight slip.

Team members siloed themselves, made autonomous decisions, and functioned without clear reporting. No documentation. No budget tracking. No guardrails. Hundreds of thousands of dollars were spent with no paper trail and no clear accountability. I wasn't lied to—but I was misled by omission. And by the time I got wind of it, we were thirty days out from the event and wildly over budget.

The result? A beautiful, seamless, high-impact event. One of our highest-rated experiences ever.

And yet success does not replace consequences. Winning does not cure rot.

When I stood in that conference room, I did what felt noble. I took full responsibility. I protected the team. I shielded the individuals from external backlash. And in doing so—I made one of the biggest leadership mistakes of my career.

I let poor performers remain. And I paid the price.

Here's what happens when you allow poor performers to stay:

- **High performers start to pull back.** They see that excellence is optional. That accountability is arbitrary. That mistakes with six-figure consequences won't result in hard decisions.

- **Cultural rot sets in quietly.** People stop raising red flags. They stop communicating. They stop caring. Not maliciously—but because the message is clear: there are no real consequences here. No one else cares, so why should they?

- **The wrong people gain influence.** Standards slip as the team starts looking to the ones who get away with things to set the standards for them, not the ones who drive results with integrity.

- **Resentment builds.** The best people feel it first. "Why am I working this hard if that person can coast, spend recklessly, miss deadlines—and still keep their job?"

This is what happens when you protect the wrong people and ignore your best team members. The team stops trusting leadership. That means they stop trusting you. The culture becomes confused. And soon enough, the walls start to crumble because the foundation has rotted from within.

I've since learned that true leadership is about creating space. If you want real feedback, don't frame the conversation. Don't lead with your opinion. Ask questions—and get out of the way.

Let them speak. Listen so you know how to lead.

WE CAN DO IT—EVEN IF WE SHOULDN'T

Not only did my desire to be liked start to infect our team internally, it bled out into our business development efforts. Our desire to be the "yes" agency, the "whatever it takes" partner, led us to skip one of the most foundational rules of agency work when we were pursuing a big piece of business: *Don't start without a contract.*

But we did just that because the client was in a rush. We thought we were being flexible.

What we were was undisciplined. I gave the go-ahead anyway, convincing myself we'd iron out the details later.

We chased another client who led us on like a toxic ex. We ignored every red flag. We were too close. Too emotionally invested. It became personal when it should have remained professional. We should've cut the cord early, but instead we let it drag out, burning time, energy, and sanity. Instead of setting appropriate boundaries, the company mirrored its founder's desire to please.

Instead of finding approval, our spinelessness invited our clients to walk all over us.

Business development is brutal. You pour your team's heart into a pitch. You bleed for an idea. And then—another loss. It's exhausting. To keep on going, you have to develop a short memory. You have to learn to fail fast. And you *must* learn to recognize toxic behavior before you agree to work for someone.

In business, as in relationships, if you're chasing one-night stands, you might get the thrill—but not the longevity. And honestly? I don't want to run a one-night-stand company. It's too hard to keep dating constantly. I want partners. Long-term. Loyal. Aligned.

If a client loves your work and wants to do business with you, they will *work* with you. They won't just string you along. If they do, are they really a partner you want to work with?

ACTION: CHECK YOUR ALIGNMENT

Success is the most seductive liar. It tells you that you're invincible. It convinces you that instincts are strategy and that momentum is mastery.

When the applause gets loud and the scoreboard is in your favor, it's easy to forget what got you there: discipline, humility, clarity, collaboration, and service.

The "I" grows louder. The listening fades. You stop questioning your assumptions because everything *seems* to be working.

That's when arrogance slips in wearing the mask of confidence, and entitlement clouds your judgment. Cracks form beneath the weight of success left unchecked.

Even though we were generating high revenue, my inability to pause and connect with my core self after my divorce—

combined with my approval-seeking, people-pleasing need to be liked, and the arrogance that pushed us forward without basic checks and balances—made the end inevitable.

I've already given you the tools to put yourself in alignment so that you don't have to spiral out of control and land in this same ugly place. No Zero Days is what took me out of it.

REFLECTION

Where is arrogance (or the idea that you deserve this) showing itself in your life? Is it in your decision making? Is it in your communication? Is it in the way you don't truly listen to those closest to you? Grab that journal and write or type your thoughts and use those thoughts to check your alignment.

CHAPTER NINE

SYSTEM FAILURE

In March, we moved into our new office, nearly 10,000 square feet of premier space. It was everything I had envisioned. Sleek. Sophisticated. Built to impress. I occupied the corner office overlooking the rolling hills of Franklin, Tennessee. It was the brand as I envisioned it, manifested in physical space. It looked like we had arrived.

But our financials betrayed a growing cancer: fool's gold.

Our P&L was inflated because of a few major projects that masked the true state of the business. We confused revenue spikes with recurring momentum. Business development wasn't prepared to sustain that level.

There was no strategy—just gut feelings and optimism. But hope isn't a strategy. And feelings don't scale.

Operationally, we had another blind spot: we failed to implement a system for scaling up or down efficiently. I had leaders, yes. Good ones. But I gave them vague goals with no deadlines, and expected flawless execution without structure.

We lacked the most basic reporting tools and performance indicators that would enable us to see what was real and what was an illusion. And worse—I wasn't stepping in to make sure we were operating with accuracy. I was too busy playing visionary in a house built on sand.

We all make mistakes. The most dangerous moment in entrepreneurship is when failure feels like winning. That's where I was, as I stood surveying our brand-new digs.

The view from the top looked impressive.

But it wasn't a summit.

It was a ledge.

IN THE RED

By late spring, I knew we had problems. After twenty years in the industry, I knew the rhythms. I understood the sales cycle. I could forecast what we needed to recover from the increases in overhead and to justify the investment in new staff, new space, and the new version of our company; everything that we'd spent to slingshot us to the next level.

Numbers don't lie. I could see we weren't even close to our monthly targets, let alone making a profit.

That month, we organized an open house to celebrate the launch of our new luxe office. We wanted the event to amplify our client base and we built an *experience* for our attendees. We crafted messaging, curated details, and poured energy into making the event feel like a *moment*.

It was supposed to be the unveiling of our new endeavors, and it was supposed to attract new clients. But as the guest list started forming, I noticed it contained the same names and faces we already knew. It was looking like we were going to have more friends in the room than prospects.

My team assured me outreach was happening—but when the day arrived and people filled the room, there was no new energy, and no new opportunities.

No new business.

I knew it the second the night ended. This event would not justify the time or the money. It was a waste and yet a waste I had to own. I saw it coming and did nothing to change it.

I could have responded right then, called an emergency meeting the very next day. I should've hit pause. I should've demanded a reset. But I didn't.

This was the opportunity I needed to step back into my business development strengths and ask the hard questions, then push for the deep answers. But I didn't.

Because doing something would mean conflict. It required tough conversations. It meant potentially removing poor performers and having them *really* not like me. I stayed passive—despite knowing the truth—because I didn't have myself centered. And because of that, my entire business spun out of control.

THROWING GOOD MONEY AFTER BAD

What did I do instead? I hired someone new—convinced they'd be the catalyst to fix everything. They'd jumpstart sales. They'd fix what wasn't working. Instead of refining systems, cutting inefficiencies, or aligning the team, I threw more weight onto an already unstable structure. It was like noticing a crack in your foundation and deciding to build a second story to stabilize it.

When things got heavy, we responded with what felt easiest—hiring. We threw people and money at the problems.

I kept underperformers out of loyalty.

We rushed others through onboarding without proper cultural or role alignment. And I framed it all under the illusion of "team responsiveness." But in truth I was afraid of saying the necessary hard things.

It was foolish. And had I been more aligned in purpose, I would have known better.

THE THREE HORSEMEN OF THE COLLAPSE

In most cases, there is no single point of failure in a business collapse—just pressure points that eventually give way. But if you're paying attention, patterns emerge.

The real catalyst wasn't a single mistake, but three critical failures that, left unaddressed, eventually broke us:

- My unchecked and unfounded confidence, which resulted in poor decisions without buy-in.

- A "like-me" culture, one that rewarded poor performers and frustrated my key players.

- A series of failures with no real consequences—my failure to provide and uphold basic business standards of measurement and accountability.

Over the course of just four months, we saw more than $1 million in losses pile up. Cash flow disappeared. The sales team was in freefall—deals weren't closing, forecasts were fiction, and the data they fed into our system was either incomplete or nonexistent. By November, I was having daily conversations about whether we could even make payroll.

Just as with my marriage, I could point my finger and blame any number of things, or I could look inward at myself.

That luxury car brand project we'd neglected to start with a contract in place? It was supposed to put us deep in the black;

instead, it became a financial black hole. It cost us over $1 million—$400,000 of it over budget—and to make matters worse, we still hadn't been paid.

Our operational systems had holes so wide that you could literally drive a truck through them. We had a $140,000 shipping mistake—oops. We issued a $200,000 credit to a client based on faulty data—oops. At the same time, we failed to book another $200,000 due from the prior December. Oops.

If you're not counting, that's a $540,000 swing just from not having clear data, sound oversight, or accountability in place.

You might wonder how I could be oblivious to all of this.

It's a fair question. On one hand, I should have known. That's what leadership demands. It's what we're supposed to do. On the other, I wasn't in a place to do it all. I hired talented people and I expected them to do their jobs—and too many of them weren't doing them well at all.

I tried convincing myself that the arrogance I'd carried through the past two years—the unchecked confidence, the belief that I could steer us through anything—*wasn't* the root of our collapse. But hindsight doesn't lie.

I'd later see with abundant clarity: My arrogance was a *big* part of the reason this was happening.

The failure was mine. I wasn't working closely enough with my direct reports. I wasn't checking the pulse of each department. I'd succumbed to the passive leadership created by the like-me culture I'd welcomed.

Most importantly—I wasn't asking the necessary hard questions.

THE HERALD OF THE END

Accountability was rotting from the inside.

In a weekly leadership meeting that October, we had just submitted a major proposal for a Fortune 500 restaurant brand. It required weekend work from a handful of key team members, including me. That wasn't the norm—we had always protected work-life balance—but this was a critical opportunity.

I opened the meeting by thanking the team and recognizing the effort. Before I could even finish, one of the employees who oversaw the weekend work raised a hand and asked, "Why did the team have to work through the weekend?"

I responded directly: "Because this proposal could change the trajectory of our Q4. It's a strategic opportunity to help us recoup losses and reposition the company."

Their response still echoes in my mind: "I'm not responsible for fixing the company's P&L. I'm responsible for protecting the team. And they worked extra hours."

There was a long pause. And then a heated exchange. But what stayed with me wasn't the disagreement—it was the mindset.

No one ever complained when the workload was light or when they took extra time off during our slower seasons. No one asked about the P&L when the perks were flowing. But the moment accountability required sacrifice, their allegiance shifted—from the company's mission to their individual comfort. That manager's response was when I knew something was really broken.

ACTION: ASK THE HARD QUESTIONS

If your team always has perfect answers, you're probably asking the wrong questions.

Hard questions sound like this:

- "Walk me through this number—what's the source, and when was it last verified?"

- "If this client doesn't pay by X date, what's our contingency plan?"

- "What's our exposure on this project, and who owns the outcome?"

- "Why are we still tolerating poor performance in this department?"

- "What data are we using to make this decision, and is it reliable?"

- "If I had to fire someone in your department tomorrow, who would it be and why?"

Those are not easy questions—but leadership isn't about comfort, it's about trust, vision, and honest communication.

REFLECTION

What hard questions are you avoiding? Take a moment and grab that journal and write down the things that come to mind. You already know what they are. Remember, no editing.

Take the one that stands out to you. Commit to ask that question this week, whether in your business or in your personal life. Start the dialogue.

CHAPTER TEN

TRIAGE

December was surreal. We hosted an extravagant Christmas party—already paid for in full earlier that year, sure—but symbolic of just how disconnected from reality we'd become. I even gave out small bonuses.

Why? What was I thinking? No one should have received a bonus. I should've canceled the party.

Deep down, I still wanted to be liked. I wanted to be known as a generous leader, even if the numbers told another story.

I naively believed that we could outrun our problems. We could out-earn, out-process, and out-hustle our way back. I still believed I could fix people's mindsets, and I cut my own pay significantly, hoping that would send a tone of solidarity. I told myself that maybe the Christmas party would help. We would return to the office in January on fire.

I believed in us. And so, although our CFO strongly advised me not to, I overruled him and deferred all my upcoming tax payments to keep $300,000 in the business so that we could make payroll.

And I'm still paying for that decision—literally. I will be for years.

What should I have done? I should have terminated those responsible for repeated failures. I should have restructured the sales team and reset compensation based on performance, not potential. I should have trimmed every excess expense, including my own.

It's easy to blame others—but the longer I looked in the mirror, the harder it became to deny: **As a leader, I'd failed. Epically.**

It was bad. But I still didn't think we'd actually sink.

And that was the problem—my oblivion was no accident. It was a defense mechanism. Somewhere between pride and exhaustion, I adopted a head-down, barrel-ahead mindset that refused to acknowledge the warning signs.

The numbers were flashing. The energy in every room was off. But I was convinced the worst was behind us. My belief? If I just performed harder, if I just pushed faster, we could outwork the unraveling.

I was wrong.

BAND-AIDS DON'T FIX BULLET HOLES

I started to live in two-week increments. Could we make it to the next cycle? Would we survive the next payroll?

Walking into the office each day felt like dragging a storm cloud through the front door. We were past triage. Every conversation felt like a collision. Every meeting was shadowed with uncertainty. I wasn't leading anymore. I was absorbing body blows.

Talks of layoffs followed our deepening financial woes. And then they became reality.

Over the previous few years, I'd faced pain from every direction. But nothing prepared me for the day I had to sit across from people I'd hired, cheered for, and invested in to tell them their positions were gone.

The expressions I saw on their faces—confusion, betrayal, disbelief—showed the kind of pain that just lingers. Heavy. Quiet. Long-lasting.

This was a test of everything I thought I knew about leadership. I had failed. We had failed. Not just the business. Not just the strategy. We failed *our people*. Their families. Their belief in us.

I know layoffs are part of business. That pruning can bring growth. That sometimes you have to throw excess weight overboard to keep the ship afloat. I understand all of that. But understanding doesn't stop the ache when you care about the people. When they're more than names on a spreadsheet.

I was gutted. These were incredible human beings. I had laughed with them, built with them, believed in them.

I went home that evening hollowed out.

And the next day—I woke up determined.

Determined not to lose again.

THE INEVITABLE END

My determination to win couldn't counter the losses that kept piling up, one after another. By April, everything we had on the table—deals we had counted on, client promises, glowing early signals—began to evaporate. There was no steadying force, no miraculous save. Just silence. Evaporation.

Some say time heals all wounds, but let me be crystal clear: Forgetting is not an option. Not for me. If I allow myself to forget, I open the door to making the same mistakes again. So, it's important for me to remember the details of my mistakes. But since I've already laid out the bones of what went wrong, I'll spare you the full, bumpy ride so that we can fast-forward out of the pain and into living with No Zero Days.

The short of it is that twelve years of building vanished in the space of twenty-one days. That's 4,380 days of effort, of leadership, of belief. Over 65,000 hours worked and countless successes undone in what felt like an instant.

The late nights, the early flights, the weekends sacrificed. Holidays skipped. Moments missed. All of it was for something I thought I believed in. Something I thought was worth bleeding for.

Advisers tried to comfort me. "You fought as hard as you could," they said. "There was nothing left to give." And maybe that's true, but it was impossible to accept.

There had to be *something* I hadn't tried, *some* path I hadn't explored. I obsessed over it—until I faced the hard truth: Even if I injected more cash (that I didn't have to inject), it would only delay the inevitable.

Somewhere between the silence and the pain, I made a decision. In a twist of cosmic irony, on the morning of Independence Day, I chose *my* independence. I had to release myself from the suffocating weight that had lived on my shoulders for the previous eighteen months.

On July 7, I met with a bankruptcy attorney. It was ominous. It was humbling. But I'm a man who moves when the decision is made. We laid out scenarios. We talked through what was next. And just for the record—it's easier to file for Chapter 7 bankruptcy than it is to finalize a divorce.

The next weeks were a blur of paperwork. All the while, I kept my team in the loop, as I'd promised I would. I truly believed we'd move past Chapter 7 together and start something new. I thought bankruptcy would be a pivot, not a death sentence. I was so naïve.

One night near the end, I had a long conversation with someone I trusted deeply—an employee who had become a friend. We talked about rebuilding together. This person said to me, "I'm in."

I hung the phone up with a touch of hopefulness for the coming days.

So, it was even more devastating twenty-four hours later when I received their resignation—via email. No conversation. No warning. Just a cold, templated message. Their email was followed by three others. Same tone. Same wording. I saw evidence of missing documents, deleted contacts, and more. Some of those I trusted most taught me a very painful and yet valuable lesson that week.

They taught me to be careful where I put my trust. In the end, human nature will look out for itself. It was misguided that I expected anything different. Reserve your inner circle for those who stay present in your life regardless of what you have to give. The world outside that circle is transactional.

Others followed. My team was dissolving. I'd built a culture based on wanting others to like me, and in the end whether or not they liked me didn't matter in the least.

On July 25, I filed the bankruptcy paperwork. The signatures were fast. The consequences? Immediate. It felt like a funeral.

No, it felt like *my* funeral. I had given twelve years and an immeasurable amount of energy to something that no longer existed. All that remained was fog. Uncertainty. And grief.

I've known darkness. But this was another level. When it was all over all I could do was crawl into bed, numb with pain. Even today I have to continually remind myself that I am not—nor will I ever be—defined by those mistakes.

Running a business is hard. It's brutal. It's lonely. It's a weight few can carry and even fewer understand. Treat yourself with some grace. We are human. And humans make mistakes. Humans fail.

But then we pick ourselves up, dust ourselves off, and reinvent our world. Our resilience is part of what makes us great.

ACTION: THE DESCENT AUDIT

You can't reverse what you won't name. This is a full confrontation of the cracks forming in your leadership, culture, and systems before they collapse underneath you. It's a gut-check, a mirror, and a mandate to lead again—this time with your eyes wide open.

There are moments when it all caves in, sometimes over just a few hard days when everything you built collapses. The weight of it hits different. You question your worth, your judgment, even who you are. Some of you have already lived through this. Others of you can feel it coming—the quiet signs you've tried to ignore, the slow drift toward burnout or denial.

If that's you, stop here. Take the time to learn what needs to change before your current course breaks you. The steps that follow are what will help you stand back up when the bottom finally gives way.

STEP 1: FACE THE FALLOUT

Write down the decisions that brought you here—the ones that still sting when you think about them. Don't edit. Don't justify. Just see them for what they are.

> ## REFLECTION
>
> What patterns are keeping you from acting sooner? What truth do you keep pushing off because it's easier to believe it will all work out?

STEP 2: AUDIT YOUR CIRCLE

Crisis has a way of showing you who's really with you. Look back at who stood by you when everything was falling apart—the ones who didn't quietly step away. That's your circle. The ones that are with you because of you, not because of how you perform.

STEP 3: REDEFINE LEADERSHIP

Leadership is about being honest, even when honesty costs you something. The hard truth is that sometimes pruning is the only way to grow again.

For example: Eliminate the things in your life that only serve to distract or remove the individuals that are not right for you and where you are going.

Why It Matters

You can't lead from exhaustion or ego. You lead from clarity. Start there.

STEP 4: REBUILD WITHOUT BITTERNESS

Pain changes people. The question is, how will it change you? Let the pain of a rebirth strip away the need to please others just so that you'll be liked, but don't let it take your capacity to care.

To help you stay centered, in your journal write one or two lines that will ground you moving forward. Something like:

I lead from what I've learned, not from what I've lost.

Now, put this somewhere where it is visible. As I have stated earlier, regret is a historical record going forward. Lean into what you have learned.

PART FOUR

LEADING FROM WHOLENESS

Two years can feel like a lifetime, but as I passed the two-year anniversary of "the end" this past summer, I leaned into a new truth about myself: I am whole.

As I've lived this journey, I have found that leading from this position has allowed me to lead with strength, with clarity, with empathy, and with the wisdom of regret.

Regret is nothing more than a historical record you can learn from.

Recently, I made a whirlwind trip across the ocean to London with a travel itinerary that would make some question my sanity, and I came back energized and inspired. What made this trip different from the thousands I've taken before?

It's that now I am whole. I am content. Everything derives from there.

Will I make more mistakes in the days ahead? Yes, absolutely. Will I see them? Will I own them? Yes, absolutely.

Leading from a place of wholeness in your pillars—for me faith is first, followed by family and, then business—is paramount to your success and to finding your No Zero Days mindset.

CHAPTER ELEVEN

SITTING IN THE RUBBLE

The morning after it all comes crashing down feels like waking in the middle of a nightmare you can't shake. You blink hard, hoping it's a bad dream. You retrace the steps, look around at the wreckage, and for a fleeting moment you wonder: *Maybe this didn't really happen.*

But it did. The weight in your chest confirms it. The silence confirms it. The phone that used to ring nonstop is now quiet. The calendar that once overflowed with meetings, travel, and deliverables? It's blank. And when you finally accept that it's real—that the implosion wasn't imagined but earned—the only question left is: *Now what?*

That's the moment I came face to face with the truth. The collapse was the cumulative result of pressure I'd put on myself to win at all costs, being disengaged from my pillars, and ignoring the warning signs.

When it finally gave way, the damage wasn't just operational—it was personal. Reputations burned. Relationships frayed. Self-worth gutted.

And yet, in the words of Elton John, I'm still standing. Not fully intact, but alive.

There's no playbook for what happens next. No checklist for waking up to a life that feels unrecognizable. The mess is too big to clean up in a day, or a week, or maybe even a year. But here's what I learned: You don't clean it all at once. You start small. You start with what's left. A breath. A journal. A phone call. A friend. A moment of clarity. One honest conversation.

You don't rebuild the old. You build something *new*—with more wisdom, more humility, and more truth.

The damage is real, but so is the opportunity. What you do now matters more than what happened then. And sometimes, rock bottom is the most honest foundation you'll ever have.

For the first time, maybe you'll stop asking how to get it all back—and start asking who you will become because of it.

STARTING FROM ZERO BUT NOT NOTHING

In a perfect world, I would have had time to breathe. Time to recover. To lick my wounds before diving back into the fight. Friends and family encouraged me to take that space. But the painful truth was, I had nothing left to rest on. No cushion. No reserve. I had poured everything into the business. Time off wasn't a luxury I could afford.

After the papers were signed, I had roughly ninety days of cash left to my name. That was it.

I remember a conversation with one of my mentors. They said, "Go back to work and fight like your life depends on it— because it actually does."

So, I did. The sun had risen on a new day and a new chapter, but the uncertainty ahead was overwhelming. Where would the business come from? How damaged was my name, my credibility? How could I rebuild from this, meet my obligations, and create something new?

I knew I needed to get back to basics. I didn't even know what the DNA of this new business was yet. But what I did know was this—checklists don't create momentum. Conversations do. Trust does.

One week later I had four make-or-break calls stacked up on a Tuesday. I remember praying that morning, "God, if You still want to be a part of my story—and me a part of Yours—I need to go four for four."

Then I got to work.

By one o'clock we had done it. Four for four. Four honest conversations about where we had been. Four potential opportunities that moved us forward.

In those early months, I didn't have time to build the perfect brand or craft polished marketing content. Having been there before I leaned on those valuable lessons I'd learned about executing with speed over perfection, but this time I also understood the value of inserting some pauses to find the best path forward.

BRICK BY BRICK

I got back to basics. Honest phone calls. Simple coffee meetings. Conversations that led to opportunity. That's how we regained traction—by being human, by being real, and by acknowledging that failure isn't final unless you let it be.

Through the years of isolation and climbing the corporate ladder I had turned my back on a lot of good people. Yet, so many of them showed up for me. One of my long-time friends met me for a coffee, and his advice to this day is part of what governs my decisions and keeps me in a place of contentment.

He asked me, "What would happen if you died tomorrow?"

"I'm worth more dead than alive," I said. "My kids would be taken care of."

"Well, if that's true, why try to rebuild Rome in a day? Retirement funds are supposed to take care of us and to leave something to our kids. If you die tomorrow and that part is already covered ... Why rush through this new beginning?"

When you've lost as much as I did, you can understand how I was tempted to rebuild *immediately*. I could have jumped right back on the hamster wheel. It seemed like the natural thing to do. Work had always been what I'd turned to; it would save me.

I believe this coffee meeting was God speaking to me, saying, *Take a breath. You have asked Me to provide for your needs, and I will do that. We will rebuild in time. Don't focus on the outcome so much that you miss the journey.*

Starting from zero isn't easy. At one point in the early Q4, I had literally $125 to my name, in TOTAL, before I was able to take my first paycheck since May of that year.

The irony? While my bank account was empty, the moments I spent alone, with friends, and with my kids were far more valuable to my heart and soul than any paycheck ever had been.

I suddenly had the freedom to enjoy late night dinners with friends I hadn't spent time with in years.

I made dates for coffee with peers and mentors. I made lunch dates with my kids and signed up for field trips.

Hearing others' stories that were not dissimilar to mine inspired me to push forward. I discovered the beauty in the struggle.

I started to see that the very situation that had caused me such pain could be helpful to someone else in ways I wouldn't have expected.

As a parent I learned one of the single most important things I needed to know: Even though I had nothing to offer materially, my kids didn't care about anything other than the fact that they were finally getting my attention. That's all they'd ever wanted.

Starting from zero is brutal. It's raw. It's not for the faint of heart. But it's possible. And I realized that if I wanted a different outcome from what had happened before, I couldn't follow the same path.

Had I chased what was familiar, I would've missed what needed to be healed. Zero isn't the end—it's just the first honest step toward becoming whole again.

FULL AUTOPSY

My hope is that, dear reader, if you find yourself in this very moment, together we can get you out of it and moving forward, in alignment with your true self.

Perhaps you are on the other side of the fence—your life isn't in chaos and things are going well—then maybe this book will serve as a reminder to you of the pitfalls that can come with that subtle, quiet drift. Regardless of where you sit in this equation, we can all benefit from a shift in mindset.

A moment of clarity can come from a variety of sources. Perhaps it was an existential experience that gave you an aha moment, or maybe it's been hitting rock bottom in the most painful way possible.

Whichever way it comes to you, I recognize that it's a real challenge to take those moments and turn them into implementable lessons.

To replace old habits or methods requires an autopsy, and that autopsy has to be nonbiased and about measurement. Data is not personal. Data is life-giving if you allow it to be.

I had to make a choice. Would I analyze to the core what went wrong? Would I blame everyone else? Would I accept my own failures?

To radically shift a mindset requires a humble approach and a willingness—no, a yearning—to sit in the mud and the mess in silent reckoning.

So how do I clean up this mess? I asked myself that question and had no answer. I had just a single day in front of me and the hope of tomorrow. So, start with what you know.

An autopsy. What a morbid word to utter. It has one association. The finality of death. But it provided me the ability to start fresh, create a new beginning. I faced the cold hard truth that anything I did next could not be a continuation of what I'd done before.

WHERE HAD I GONE ASTRAY?

One of the greatest lessons I've learned is that pausing to think and reflect is one of the most strategic tools you have access to, even if it feels counterintuitive to fast movers like us.

I took a few days and kept them free of forward motion. I didn't make any calls or chase any opportunities. I sat in silence and thought about the mess I had made. I started to write.

In the end, I came up with a sobering list.

- **Arrogance:** This was a big one. It was harder to see initially because I was never an outwardly arrogant guy. I gave credit to my team, but behind closed doors I believed I was invincible.

- **Failed Priorities:** My priorities were increasingly out of alignment. I measured my success by growth in our business, not by growth as a man, father, or leader. I had no idea how to relentlessly move forward as an entrepreneur and still be the kind of man I needed to be. In the absence of know-how, I invested in what was easy: work and work only.

- **Leadership:** I abandoned key areas without setting a roadmap. I failed to cultivate growth through conversation and accountability.

- **Finance:** We talked for years about rebuilding the financial backbone of the company but kept applying Band-Aids. By the time we improved our data, it was too late.

- **Accountability:** I absorbed all the blame. But as one team member told me, "That's noble, but your failure wasn't in taking the blame—it was in not demanding results from the people hired to deliver them."

- **Like-Me Culture:** I let the desire to be liked cloud my good judgment. I made decisions to garner approval and neglected to tend to the outcomes of my approval-seeking, especially among staff.

- **Abandoning My Strengths:** I handed off the most important aspects of our company—the very areas I was strongest in—so I could pursue what I *wanted* to do, not what I *should* have done.

An autopsy shows you many things, and, most importantly, you discover this truth: No one is irreplaceable, including you. The business will move on without you. Your family will move on without you.

If this second act was going to work, I had to address these issues head-on and without bias.

WHAT NEEDED TO CHANGE?

The autopsy gave way to identifying what healthy looks like.

HUMILITY

Nothing has humbled me quite like having everything taken away from me and having my very survival put into question.

I spent a LOT of time in self-examination—tracing how I'd strayed from my roots, what led me to believe that I was invincible and could stop learning, and why I thought I'd somehow reached the pinnacle of success.

Before any other change could take root, I had to start with my core inner soul and answer a profound question: What was active humility versus passive humility? There certainly is a difference.

Active humility is not deferring to everyone else at the cost of your own voice. It is not taking blanket responsibility for any and all given situations. It is not a split posture on what you show outwardly versus what you feel inside.

Active humility means living with an open hand and an open mind. It requires active, engaged listening and an equal measure of observation. Active humility prioritizes service. Active humility means you are continually seeking to learn. It requires admitting when you are wrong and gracefully holding the line when you are right.

Passive humility is marked by deferral and reactivity. Life happens to you. Passive humility is a guise that you hide behind when you are uncomfortable in your own skin. It is easier to play the martyr than to find your voice and embrace it.

If life is happening to you, there is always a scapegoat that isn't you. You are humble but not humbled. After all, if there is always someone or something on the other end of your finger-pointing, then you never have to accept true responsibility. As a result, growth cannot and will not ensue.

The epiphany and shift toward active humility gave me an inner strength I didn't know it was possible to possess. It allowed me to have true clarity, new vision, and, most importantly, the ability to accept where I'd gone wrong.

Understanding this difference allows me to see that each day and each win is a gift. I have the reserves to help when I see someone who needs help. I am able to seek out and learn from those who are smarter than me. I invest in the next generation of entrepreneurs, while openly admitting my own failures and never being afraid to do so.

NEW PRIORITIES

I knew my priorities would have to change for good. I'd sat on the sidelines of complete destruction and forced myself to see the complete path of the storm. It became very clear: My priorities would need to be reorganized and non-negotiable or I'd run the risk of being back in the same place all over again.

My pillars are my priorities. They aren't something I set and forget. They require daily, weekly, and monthly gut checks: *Am I in alignment?*

Life comes at us fast, and it is easier than ever before to get distracted chasing the shiny new thing or simply to get off track. Today, I can sense when my priorities have veered off path. I have learned not to expect perfection, but rather to rely on my new awareness to make quick adjustments.

I make sure to listen to my intuition instead of silencing it. Our body has a unique way of communicating to us, whether it's that blah feeling when you haven't worked out for a few days or that turn in your stomach that says, *This is not who I am.* Listen to it and return to what works.

Listen to that voice. Don't ignore it. Don't allow yourself to become comfortable with the inner angst you feel when you're adrift from your pillars. Comfort leads to complacency, which leads to your world turning upside down, the opposite of your true desires.

LEADERSHIP

Strength and humility are best when harmonized. To be a stronger leader, I needed to redefine the role for myself. To do this, I first identified and recognized my strengths, and then I embraced them.

My prime directive now is to define the *what* and the *why* of what we're doing, and then to empower my team to figure out the *how*. I leaned back into what I do best: building relationships and business development. I keep my hand on the pulse to ensure we collectively stay aligned and I course-correct fast. In other words, I am an engaged leader.

With my family, my job is to lead with purpose, to live as an example of a man of faith, and also to listen to my daughters' small voices as they tell me with no filter what they really need from me.

Today, I lead from a place of confidence, grounded in self-awareness and humility. I've changed. I've set new boundaries.

I still value relationships, but they're no longer built on a need to be liked. They're built on truth, performance, shared vision, and most importantly, mutual respect.

I'm no longer trying to earn approval. I'm motivated by purpose, not insecurity. I'm driven to serve, to listen and to learn from my team, those close to me, and those that inspire me.

I've reclaimed the parts of me that were lost in the chaos, and in so doing I've found the ability to be truly present for those in my life.

Rather than sitting in the ashes of my failures, I now celebrate them for the refinement they've brought to my leadership style. Without the failures, I wouldn't be here.

FINANCES

I have learned not to make decisions based on hope. In my new venture, we work from data, even when it is unpleasant and doesn't show us what we want to see. Data is not personal; it removes all of the emotion from decisions. As humans, we are prone to emotion-based decision making. Clean data is the key to making truly sound, informed decisions.

In designing the new venture, I shared our business model with outside experts and asked them to design a system with two goals: (1) Give us high visibility into real data, and (2) make us sellable. Whether we sell or not doesn't matter. A sellable business is typically a healthy business, so seeking to be sellable was a way of ensuring we would be operating cleanly.

With high visibility and real data, we are informed. Every decision now ties back to our North Star—it's measurable, benchmarked, and intentional.

If I could go back in time and fix only one thing, I would have started the business with a seller's mindset. You may be in a business you love, or you may be thinking about starting a business, and the idea of selling may be laughable. I get it.

I assumed I would build a company and run it until I retired. A natural desire, but it was grounded in the wrong principles. As an owner/founder, your relationship with your P&L changes if you have no end game. Start with an end game, no matter how crazy it seems, and build from there. You will thank yourself later.

MEASUREMENT (NOT ACCOUNTABILITY)

I replaced the word *accountability* with *measurement*. Accountability feels personal to this current workforce and seems to dismiss what a team is doing well when trying to correct the things they are not.

Measurement is objective. We can measure our successes as well as our failures without emotion. Evaluations and decisions should be based on cold hard data—whether we like it or not—because up-to-date data rarely lies.

This shift is not surface level or only in the words you use. It requires instituting processes that provide the data to measure.

We now measure everything—effort vs. time, performance, outcomes, alignment. Measurement does not eliminate hard conversations. Measurement removes ego from the conversation and keeps our team focused on progress, not blame.

CULTURE

I stopped trying to manufacture culture with perks and fun.

> I'VE LEARNED THAT STRONG TEAMS WANT VISION, TRANSPARENCY, LEADERSHIP, AND CONSISTENCY.

None of those are found in team outings, expensive dinners, or lush office spaces, etc. You can have all of those things and still have a culture that rots from the inside out. My story as Exhibit A shows that.

You need all four of them to be successful with consistency being the most important. Make every effort to do what you say you are going to do, and if there comes a time when you are unable to follow through, then be upfront and transparent in your communication.

My job is to be the steady current that flows underneath the choppy surface of my company, allowing my leadership team to shape a culture that sticks. Yes, it starts with me—but not in the way I once thought.

When I am honest with myself, all of the personas I've developed over the years—the ones I used to subconsciously try to maintain all day, every day—are stripped away. I'm left with my core self. My pillars.

When you focus your energy on maintaining your masks, it is nearly impossible to see when you are off course. You're wearing them only because you don't quite trust that people will love you for who you are, not what you do. It's possible you feel numb and are in the grip of the quiet drift.

Strip all of those masks away and you'll notice the subtle changes. You'll notice a feeling in your soul that something isn't quite right. In relationships with your partner, in relationships with your kids, and in business, the smallest weekly variance can spiral if you're not paying attention. You can't wait for the fix—you have to become the fix. You address issues quickly. You correct yourself confidently, trusting that you are worthy of being appreciated and loved for who you are, not just what you do.

ACTION: CUT YOURSELF OPEN

These next four steps are about one word: **honesty.**

Honesty with yourself. Honesty with others.

My autopsy was all I had left. I was left for dead—on the table. So, the only way out was through deep and raw analysis. If you find yourself in this spot, dig deep into the action steps below.

And for some of you, maybe the worst hasn't happened … yet. Maybe you see it coming. If that's you, let's conduct a *living autopsy* before a crash comes.

STEP 1: FACE THE RUINS (OR IMAGINE THEM)

Whether the collapse already came or still lives only in your imagination, face it.

If it's already happened, acknowledge the truth of what fell apart and why.

If it hasn't, visualize the worst-case scenario—the business, the relationship, the identity that could crumble if you keep ignoring the warning signs.

Pain, real or imagined, is a teacher. Don't look away.

> ### REFLECTION
>
> If everything collapsed today, what part of your life or leadership would you most regret neglecting?

STEP 2: PERFORM THE AUTOPSY

Autopsies reveal cause, not blame.

Look without defensiveness. In either scenario—the one that happened or the one you want to avoid—dissect the habits, assumptions, and blind spots that brought you here or could bring you down.

Do you have blind spots in any of these?

- Culture and conflict?

- Finances?

- Leadership?

- Accountability?

Write what you discover as data, not drama. You're the observer, not the victim.

List the top three "causes of death" in your last collapse or the three pressure cracks you can already see forming if you don't make changes now.

STEP 3: LEAD WITH ACTIVE HUMILITY

Autopsies are worthless if pride writes the report.

Active humility means you're open to being wrong, to learning again, to leading differently.

In crisis, humility reveals character; in prevention, it builds endurance.

Choose to be teachable before you're forced to be.

Revisit the autopsy you've prepared and ask yourself what it's missing. What weren't you prepared to put on the page the first time? Put it there now.

Why It Matters

Active humility turns pain into progress. It keeps your ego from rewriting the story before you've learned the lesson.

STEP 4: REBUILD BRICK BY BRICK

Now, start where you are—with what's left, or what's worth keeping.

Then take one positive action. One call. One meeting over coffee. One small, new discipline. Don't try to restore what you had—what you already know doesn't work. Now you're going to focus on constructing something truer and more durable.

Whether you're rising from wreckage or averting it, it doesn't matter how small the next step you take is, as long as you take it.

CHAPTER TWELVE

RISING FROM THE ASHES

There were two noticeable differences that emerged in my life shortly after that painful finality: the death of my business and, before that, the death of my marriage.

First, was my faith. I came to a place where I had nowhere else to turn. I had friends and family, sure, but the reality is that the only way out of this was to turn back to my faith and recognize that there is a God who loves me despite all of my failures.

To be completely transparent, when I started to rekindle my relationship with God, I wasn't convinced it would work, but what else did I have to lose?

I've lived through dark days and made it through to the other side. And today, my life is a living example of what it looks like when God shows up.

Though I had long distanced myself from the faith I was raised in, something shifted. I sat empty-handed in my living room that August, said a clumsy, desperate prayer—and God was there. Instantly. I was the one who had drifted. He had never left.

I later told a friend: "He was only a morning prayer away."

I'll mark that day every year to celebrate the beginning of my second chapter.

In addition to rediscovering my faith, for the first time in my life I was living a life that was entirely my own.

LIFE IN TECHNICOLOR, OR THE DOPAMINE RESET

For most of the previous decade the world had gone gray. The colors had drained out of my life so slowly that I barely noticed, until one day when I woke up and realized I hadn't really felt *anything* in a very long time. Not joy. Not sorrow. Not hope. Just … numbness.

I've learned there's a scientific reason for this feeling—a biological explanation for why stress strips the color out of living. It starts with dopamine. This small but mighty neurotransmitter fuels motivation, reward, and our ability to find pleasure in the world around us. It's the chemical spark that makes us notice how the morning sunlight paints gold across a wooden floor, or how our child's laughter rings out like music, or how closing a big deal sends a surge of purpose through our chest. Dopamine is, in many ways, the pigment that colors life.

But under the weight of chronic stress, dopamine begins to vanish. Prolonged pressure triggers a surge of stress hormones like cortisol, flooding our systems until the brain's dopamine circuits become overloaded and, eventually, depleted. Studies show that chronic stress can lower dopamine production, reduce the sensitivity of dopamine receptors, and blunt the brain's ability to feel pleasure at all. This is why, during seasons of relentless strain, everything begins to feel flat. We stop noticing the small joys. The little details that once sparkled fade into background noise. Even good news lands with a dull thud. The highs disappear, but so do the lows, leaving us suspended in a colorless purgatory of emotional neutrality.

This state has a name: anhedonia—the inability to experience pleasure. But for many of us, it feels less clinical and more existential.

It's the *quiet drift* I wrote about earlier. You're going through the motions, nodding in meetings, tucking your kids into bed, carrying out conversations with clients or colleagues. Outwardly, your life might even look successful.

But inside, there's a war you can't name. The absence of feeling becomes its own private torture. And the scariest part is how easily you can convince yourself this is normal, this is just what adulthood feels like.

For me, this drift grew so subtle that I didn't even realize how far I'd gone. I no longer noticed the way my daughter's eyes sparkled when she showed me something new she'd learned. I stopped hearing laughter in a crowded room as an invitation to be a part of the group.

I was alive, but I wasn't *living*. And in my business, I'd lost the sharp clarity that had always guided my decisions. Everything blurred together into one exhausting gray.

But here's the truth: it doesn't have to stay that way. As clinical research shows, the brain has an incredible capacity for healing. The same neural pathways that went dim under stress can light up again.

Dopamine systems can regenerate. Neuroplasticity is our saving grace. Yet the road back isn't instantaneous—it often takes weeks or even months for those circuits to reset. Studies suggest that even after prolonged stress, if we remove the sources of strain and begin living differently, dopamine levels can begin to rebound within four to twelve weeks. Slowly, life regains its color.

And when it does, it's as if someone has taken a cloth and wiped a film from the glass. You start noticing small things again.

The laughter of your kids becomes a song you want to dance to. The way sunlight filters through the trees stops you in your tracks. In business, you see clearly once more—the risks and the rewards, the nuance between pros and cons. The numbness gives way to feeling. Not just the good stuff—joy, excitement, gratitude—but also the hard things: fear, sadness, vulnerability. Yet even those feel more bearable than the suffocating void of apathy.

When dopamine returns to balance, you find yourself in a place of admission, acknowledging that the quiet drift was slowly killing you from the inside out. It takes courage to admit how disconnected you've become, to face the cost of living without feeling. But there's also relief in it, because the pain of feeling is a sign that you're still alive. And being alive—truly alive—is worth everything.

It took some time, but the world came into full color again. Uncertainty was at an all-time high. I had no idea what was coming next, but I no longer had to wear all those exhausting masks. I no longer had to stretch myself thin. Pretty soon, my body remembered how to sleep without stress or insomnia. I finally slept with peace. It had probably been two decades since that had happened.

FIRST FOCUS

Starting again requires a focused discipline. Your first inclination might be to apply that discipline to the business you're starting, but that wouldn't have worked; I'd have ended up in the same place all over again. I needed to focus that discipline on *me* first.

My heart. *My* soul. *My* mental mindset. *My* physical body.

I have found that when I first take two to three hours a day for myself, I am a better leader, business owner, human, and, most importantly, a better and more present father.

I'll still work long hours; it's in my blood. But with focus, those long hours possess a 3x output over working from a place of pure exhaustion. There is no glory in exhaustion, despite what we have been taught to believe.

At first, these hours for me created the space to begin the process of rewiring everything I thought I knew about myself (and to stop wondering or caring so much what others thought about me). The window of quiet and the nonjudgmental safety of my journal allowed my thoughts to flow freely as I relentlessly asked myself question after question.

My answers didn't come overnight, but they did come, and as they did, they slowly paved the way for a radical paradigm shift.

In that space, all of the personas I'd projected over the years were gone. All that was left was me. Just me. Justin Zebell. I craved this time. My spirit demanded this time.

MIND THE GAP

My routine became non-negotiable, with one catch. The word *grace* is paramount. I won't achieve a perfect day every day (and truthfully, if I did, then I'm not reaching high enough). There will be gaps. But I won't let those gaps turn into chasms.

I'd learned over the summer how present I needed to be for my kids. For the first time in a long time, my vision was clear. I went back to work open handed. I knew I had done this before, and with the proper perspective I could do it again.

But my new perspective was tested almost immediately when an acquaintance shared a job posting with me and offered to set up the next steps for me.

The listing described my dream job with one of the most recognizable brands in the world. It was right up my alley. I'd be a jetsetter, living in New York for two weeks a month and

Nashville for the other two. I would travel the world doing what I do best. Financially it would be more than enough to sustain me AND it was a cool job.

I considered it for about half a day and then declined to pursue it. It didn't fit my long-term vision. I had no idea what my real long-term vision was other than I wanted to be a dad and a human first and an entrepreneur second. And if I'd applied to that job, I'd already be betraying myself.

I chose a new paradigm, and I keep choosing it. Every day. No Zero Days.

ACTION: SIT IN THE SHADOWS

You don't need all the answers right now. But you do need to start telling yourself the truth. Because that's how you begin to clear the debris and make room for a new path forward built on humility, new priorities, and the freedom to be fully yourself.

That's the real gold at the end of the rainbow we've been chasing. And we can get to it, with a little effort.

STEP 1: EMBRACE THE QUIET RESET

It wasn't until it was all stripped away that I was forced to embrace the quiet. What I feared most is what I now find myself craving. That didn't come overnight. It came with practice. The practice of listening to the healthy voice in the quiet. If you learn to embrace the quiet reset, you will look forward to those moments of silence.

> ## REFLECTION
>
> My challenge to you is this: Take one hour this week to sit in quiet and write down the truths you've been avoiding.
> Where have you been arrogant?
> Where have your priorities slipped out of alignment?
> Where have you handed off your strengths or hidden behind busyness because it's safer than admitting you're scared or unsure?

I know that this is a challenge because we like to focus on our next win, not our last loss. But unless we embrace the shadow, we'll never see the light.

STEP 2: RECONNECT BEFORE YOU RE-ENGAGE

Before you rebuild anything external, recalibrate the internal. For me, it started with faith—a morning prayer whispered through exhaustion. For you, it might be gratitude, stillness, or simply sitting with what hurts until you can name it.

Don't rush your comeback. Let it form from conviction.

Spend fifteen minutes each morning this week alone—no phone, no soundtrack, no external voices from podcasts or the radio. Just breathe and listen. Find comfort in being alone with your thoughts.

STEP 3: RESET THE CHEMISTRY

Stress steals color from life by burning through your brain's dopamine. The cure is found in boundaries you set for yourself and others. Here are some examples:

1. Don't look at your email or slack until 8 a.m. or after you have invested in yourself.

2. Use any number of apps or solutions to manage your social media time and turn it off at a time of day that works for you. I personally use Brick and have listed it in Resources.

3. Turn off the noise and leave space at the beginning and end of your day to reflect and slow down your heart rate.

Reclaim the small moments that once brought you joy.

Let your body and mind remember what peace feels like. Over time, the color returns—one sunrise, one laugh, one quiet win at a time.

Why It Matters

Healing your dopamine system is strategic recovery and without it you'll always feel depleted, like you're running on fumes and don't have the energy to fully engage. Clarity, creativity, and leadership all depend on your ability to feel again.

STEP 4: BUILD FROM THE SHADOWS

You'll know you're ready to re-emerge when you no longer need to prove anything. Until then, stay low. Protect the discipline that got you here.

When you finally step back into the light—with new ideas, new ventures, and new energy—let it be a surprise to those you used to seek approval from. You don't need validation when you've already done the work.

Outline your new rhythm—build it around your pillars. For me, it's faith, family, business, and my future, which requires me to be emotionally and physically healthy. Guard those hours fiercely. Progress made in the dark becomes power in the light.

CHAPTER THIRTEEN

NO ZERO DAYS ARRIVES FOR YOU

Wherever you're standing right now—in chaos or in calm—pause long enough to look honestly at the road you're on. Do your priorities still serve the life you want to build? Are you drifting or deciding? Are you leading, or hiding behind old habits and personas you no longer need?

I've learned the hard way that rebuilding a business—or a life—is about looking into the mess without flinching, performing your own honest autopsy, and figuring out what needs to be left behind so something healthier can take its place.

I've already told you about the advent of No Zero Days and how it crystallized my healing process. I want the same forward motion for you.

THE NO ZERO DAYS MENTALITY

No Zero Days marks the beginning of a new commitment. No Zero Days means you show up every day and take action—even if it's small—and stay present in the process. No Zero Days is about consistent forward motion toward a version of yourself you haven't met yet—your most authentic self.

Maybe this feels too simple. The concept is simple—but the action, like anything that matters, takes intentionality. *No Zero Days* is built on defining your pillars and interacting with those pillars every day. They become the voice that guides your decisions and your progress.

For me, everything after faith and family connects back to my business ventures, my hobbies, and my passions. When I'm with my kids, that pillar requires me to be fully present with them. I put the phone down, listen, laugh, and *show up*. In business, it's leading with purpose, creating with clarity, and pushing forward even when it's uncomfortable. In my passions, it's making space to build, move, or create; whatever fills the tank that day.

Each moment, I focus on the pillar that matters most in the space I'm in and maximize my investment, no matter how big or small the step feels compared to the day before. That's what *No Zero Days* really means.

You don't have to navigate this alone, or perfectly. What matters is that you keep moving—one day, one choice, one action at a time.

OWNING THE WHOLE YOU

Just Do It.

Dare to Dream.

Think Different.

Seize the Day.

I'm sure you recognize these taglines. They are deceptively simple in their form because their meaning can be transformational. If you are an athlete, maybe *Just Do It* gives you the motivation you need to fit in a late-night workout, do extra reps in the gym, or power through a grueling race. You adopt the concept because it helps you. Their brand helps to form your identity.

If you adopt No Zero Days, I challenge you to own your identity. Aligning yourself with your three pillars creates a fundamental shift that has nothing to do with whether you are wearing a certain shoe, quoting literary pieces from a stage, or building the next great tech.

Finding your authenticity might require deep breaths, long exhales, understanding of you as a person to the core, and most importantly, finding love in your heart for who you *are*. You matter apart from what you create and build.

Own your brand, commit to No Zero Days, and with that as your foundation, know that you are more than equipped to lead the next great movement, generate the next great innovation, and inspire the next great generation of leaders.

UNDERSTANDING AND LOVING YOURSELF

I've learned to offer myself compassion. I've learned that it's okay to ask for help, to lean on others. Admitting that I am a work in progress? That's okay, too. My worth is not defined by my wins or failures. I am enough as I am.

I didn't get here overnight. It took work.

This year, like that year, my kids are with me. And just like that summer, it was their smiles, their laughter, and their presence that saved me. They didn't care about money or trips or things. They cared about me. They wanted *presence*—mine. Much in the same way God did. I didn't have to do anything. I am enough as I am.

So are you.

LIVING A NO ZERO DAYS LIFE

So what happens when you live with No Zero Days? A lot.

I found myself. It's a version of me that's taken forty-six years to fully meet.

I became the father I'd always wanted to be. I watched my daughters grow and flourish. I laughed freely—then laughed some more.

I stopped worrying about being liked and started simply being *me*. I rebuilt broken relationships. I watched God reward slow faith—not with speed, but with precision. He placed an unexpected gift in front of me and said, *"Watch. Wait."* And I am. And it's worth waiting for.

I watched a new venture thrive beyond expectations. I wrote. Then I wrote some more. I saw new people enter my life right on time—people who showed up and stood tall. I discovered what pure joy really feels like, and how much joy there is in seeing others shine. I was reminded of my true purpose—and how simple it actually is. I learned the beauty of cutting out the excess and seeing clearly what remains. I focused on my spiritual, mental, and physical health. I made more time for people—and somehow, found more time in the day. I embraced the simple. I made memories with my kids. And then made more. I relearned how to love—and what grace looks like in real time. I didn't lose my house. I never missed a meal.

I could go on—blessing after blessing, quiet lesson after quiet lesson. But some are for my heart only, and for those closest to me. Maybe someday they'll find their way into another book.

One year ago, I prayed: *God, if you want to be part of my story—then write one that only You could write.*

And He did.

As I sit here today, reflecting on the last twenty-four months—and the years that led to them—I feel nothing but gratitude.

Gratitude for the pain that shaped me. Gratitude for the growth that followed. Gratitude for the grace that held me.

I am strong. I am resilient. I am loving. I am learning to live with intention, to be present, to savor the moments. I am learning to be content.

I live with No Zero Days.

DEFINE YOUR RESURRECTION

Resurrection is about embracing your new identity. You're not the same person you were before. You've grown, evolved, and discovered new depths of your potential. You've shed old patterns and limiting beliefs, and you've embraced your authentic self.

This stage is a new beginning, a launchpad for future adventures, and a foundation for you to have even greater impact. You're now equipped to face new challenges with confidence, wisdom, and a deep understanding of yourself.

Resurrection is about bringing your full self to the world, integrating all aspects of your being—your strengths, your vulnerabilities, and your experiences—into your entrepreneurial endeavors. It's about living and leading with intention, purpose, and authenticity. It's about continuing to grow, learn, and evolve, knowing that the journey never truly ends.

It begins every day with a commitment to No Zero Days.

So, embrace your resurrection, step into your new role, and continue to create, innovate, and inspire. Your story is far from over; it's just entered a powerful new chapter.

ACTION: COMMIT TO NO ZERO DAYS

STEP 1: REFLECT ON YOUR JOURNEY

You've walked through the drift, the rebuilding, and the re-discovery of who you really are.

Now, it's time to name what *No Zero Days* means for you.

We've been through a lot together in these pages, and I hope my stories have helped you to see your own story more clearly. Reflect on what you've learned and write down:

- **Three truths** you've discovered about yourself.
- **Two shifts** you've made or are ready to make.
- **One defining moment** when you realized you were done living on autopilot.

Now, decide. How will you *step into* No Zero Days—not as a slogan, but as a way of life?

What will it look like for you to live with intention, build with purpose, and move forward one day at a time?

STEP 2: RECLAIM WHAT'S YOURS

The old version of you played to please others in order to try to stay safe. That season is over.

Everything you've learned through this book has been preparing you to reclaim your identity and your purpose.

List your **three core pillars**—the foundations of who you are.

For each, write one daily action that honors it.

STEP 3: LEAD YOURSELF WITH GRACE

You've learned to build, lead, and serve others.

Now, lead yourself—with grace. You deserve to let go of shame or blame or feeling like a failure. You are not your past.

No Zero Days is about presence and consistency, not perfection.

Consider the following prompts and then write down your authentic responses to them:

- Write one sentence beginning with: *I am enough because...*

- Describe one way you'll extend grace to yourself the next time you stumble or stall.

REFLECTION

What would change if you spoke to yourself the way you speak to the people you love most?

Why It Matters

Consistency is important; it's part of emotional regulation. But so is compassion. Without it even the strongest leaders burn out. Grace keeps you moving when motivation fades. It's important to learn to give yourself the grace you deserve. You do deserve it, and with time you can learn to recognize that, if you don't already.

STEP 4: THE NO ZERO DAYS DECLARATION

You've done the work. You've faced your past and reclaimed your purpose.

Now you stand in the space between who you were and who you're becoming.

This is your resurrection. Your daily renewal.

Print this. Sign it. Own it.

For me, No Zero Days means showing up—
fully and faithfully—
every single day that I can.

It also means taking one intentional action,
however small, toward becoming
who I'm meant to be
when that's all that I can do.

No Zero Days means building with purpose,
leading with heart, and creating
from a place of alignment, not fear.

Living with intention will give me peace,
clarity, and strength.

Today, I commit to a life of No Zero Days.

Signature: _______________________________

Date: _______________________________

CHAPTER FOURTEEN

HONESTY IS POWER

When you're an entrepreneur, the highs are exhilarating—and the lows can be soul-crushing. If you're reading this, it's likely you've been on that ride. You've risked everything. You've woken up at 2 a.m. with your heart pounding, wondering if you'll make payroll. You've also stood in rooms feeling ten feet tall, closing the deal that changes your trajectory.

And if you've landed here—living life by the principle of No Zero Days—you know that the real power isn't just in the wins. It's in the story you carry. It's in the honesty with which you tell it.

I tell my story at least ten times a week. Sometimes over coffee, sometimes on a stage, sometimes quietly across the dinner table with someone who's on the brink of their own implosion. And here's what I've discovered: the more honest I am about what happened—the missteps, the chaos, the moments I doubted myself—the more community I build around me.

Because honesty is magnetic.

We live in a world starved for authenticity. We scroll past curated highlight reels all day, craving something real. Something human. When you share your honest truth, you become a mirror for others. You give them permission to be honest about their own struggles. And in that space of shared truth, real community forms.

Living with No Zero Days isn't just about big leaps forward. It's about the small, gritty details. It's waking up and admitting:

- "Today I'm exhausted and my mind is scattered."

- "I'm terrified this idea might fail."

- "I feel like an imposter in this room."

- "I'm proud of how I handled that hard conversation."

Be honest about what's hard. Be honest about the days you get off track. Because pretending everything is perfect is the fastest way to isolation. And there's nothing more powerful—or freeing—than being real.

Your honesty might be the exact thing someone else needs to hear. It might save their business. Or their marriage. Or simply remind them that they're not alone.

ACTION: TELL YOUR STORY

There is power in your story. I tell mine all the time, and it brings connection and serves to recenter me. This week, I challenge you to:

- Tell your story to one person, fully and honestly.

- Speak the hard truth, even if your voice shakes.

- Let the people closest to you know how you're really feeling.

There is nothing more authentic—or more powerful—than living with intention and living honestly. And that is what No Zero Days is all about.

NO ZERO DAYS, NO GOING BACK

If you've made it here, to the end of *No Zero Days*, I hope I've persuaded you to choose a path of relentless forward motion, refusing to let any day slip away untouched by progress, no matter how small.

But don't forget this: There's just as much power in your honesty as in your hustle. No Zero Days isn't about mindlessly crossing items off a to-do list—it's about the raw truth you're willing to acknowledge about yourself and your commitment to hold fast to your authenticity.

If there's one thing I've learned, it's that the journey of building a life, a business, or a dream is never a straight line. It's filled with highs that make you feel unstoppable—and lows that make you question everything. And the glue that holds it all together is honesty. The willingness to say, "I'm struggling today." Or "I'm terrified this might fail." Or even "I'm proud of what I've built."

Every day, you're faced with a simple question: *Is today a No Zero Day?* And you find a way to say, "Yes."

Living with No Zero Days is an everyday practice. It's built in inches and moments. It's embedded in the decision you make to keep moving—and to keep telling your story honestly, even when your voice shakes.

As you walk this path, remember, momentum matters. But so does the truth. The real power lies in choosing to live each moment with intention, and the courage to speak your honest, human story along the way. That's what No Zero Days is all about.

INDELIBLE INK

You don't need a tattoo on your arm that reads "No Zero Days" to move forward with intention.

But I chose to put one there anyway.

Those three small words are inked where I can see them every day. Others can see them, too. It's not there for decoration—it's a reminder. A compass.

Because the truth is, No Zero Days isn't a one-time mantra you write in a journal and forget. It's not a slogan you slap on a T-shirt and leave in your closet. It's an everyday practice.

Every single day.

Each moment is made up of the decisions you make. And in each moment, there's a question waiting to be asked:

Is today a No Zero Day?

It doesn't have to be monumental. Some days, my "No Zero" might be five minutes of journaling when I'm dead tired. A phone call I'd been avoiding. A new idea scratched on a napkin. A workout, even if it's just ten push-ups on my living room floor.

Other days, it's being fully present with my kids and blocking everything else out. It's building a company, starting a foundation. Writing a book. Forgiving someone—or myself.

I can't count the times people have stopped me because they noticed the tattoo.

The attendant scanning tickets at the Empire State Building, leaning in closer to read my arm.

The woman I stood next to in London at the Coldplay show leaned over and asked me, "What does that mean?"

Friends I haven't seen in years who spot it often ask, "What's that about?"

The person sitting next to me on the shuttle bus to the airport, catching a glimpse and striking up a conversation.

They all ask.

They want to know what it means.

And when they ask, it reminds me all over again. It forces me to define it, to say it out loud. And in saying it, I recommit to it.

When I'm stuck—mentally, emotionally, professionally—I look down and see those three words.

No Zero Days.

It's my cue to recalibrate. To remember that action—even small action—breaks the inertia. That progress is built in inches and minutes, not just in leaps and milestones.

So I started a No Zero Day Challenge.

Not for the world. For me.

Today, I'll do one thing that moves me forward. One thing that matters, no matter how small. One thing that makes sure the scoreboard doesn't read "zero."

That's it. That's the secret.

No Zero Days isn't about perfection. It's about momentum. It's about refusing to let days slip away untouched by effort, untouched by intention.

You don't need a tattoo to live this way.

But I have mine.

And every day, it asks me the same question:

Is today a No Zero Day?

And every day, I answer.

Yes.

FINAL THOUGHTS

Thank you for giving your time and walking with me on this journey. I hope parts of my story have offered something meaningful: lessons you can learn from, and maybe a few that help you avoid some of the pain and challenges that came with mine.

While this book was written from my perspective as an entrepreneur, the No Zero Days mindset isn't limited to business. Whether you're a student, a stay-at-home parent, entering your twilight years, or somewhere in between, there's always time to start again with a new mindset—one built on intentional living.

Call it No Zero Days. Or call it something else.

Whatever you do, live your life to the fullest. Find the process or idea that resonates with you. We only get one life and a finite number of moments.

Make the most of them. No Zero Days.

TOOLS AND RESOURCES

PODCASTS

1. **The Diary of a CEO – Steven Bartlett**
   Self-awareness, internal tension, and the real cost of growth.

2. **How I Built This – Guy Raz**
   Founder stories that normalize collapse, rebuilds, and resilience.

3. **The Knowledge Project – Shane Parrish**
   Mental models, decision-making, and long-term leadership discipline.

4. **The Ryan Leak Podcast**
   Failure, humility, and leadership practiced daily

5. **The Craig Groeschel Leadership Podcast**
   Systems, team development, and leading at scale.

ENNEAGRAM RESOURCES

1. **The Road Back to You – Ian Morgan Cron & Suzanne Stabile**
   An accessible and practical starting point, especially useful for teams.

2. **The Wisdom of the Enneagram – Don Richard Riso & Russ Hudson**
   The definitive reference on motivations, stress paths, and growth trajectories.

3. **Personality Types – Don Richard Riso**
   Deep insight into leadership behavior under pressure.

4. **The Enneagram in Love & Work – Helen Palmer**
   Practical application for communication, conflict, and team dynamics.

5. **The Enneagram Institute**
   Ongoing digital reference for levels of health, leadership patterns, and integration.

LEADERSHIP & ENTREPRENEURSHIP BOOKS

1. *Chasing Failure* – **Ryan Leak**
   Reframes failure as a teacher and momentum engine.

2. *The Hard Thing About Hard Things* – **Ben Horowitz**
   An honest operator's manual for leadership under pressure.

3. *Elon Musk* – **Walter Isaacson**
   A case study in vision, first-principles thinking, intensity, and tradeoffs at scale.

4. *Extreme Ownership* – **Jocko Willink & Leif Babin**
   Accountability without loopholes. Leadership without excuses.

5. *The 12 Week Year* – **Brian Moran**
   Execution discipline that compresses time and eliminates drift.

BOOK JUSTIN TO SPEAK

Justin's keynote presentations include:

• No Zero Days: Living with Intention–
The foundational philosophy and three pillars framework

• Leading from Wholeness: Beyond the Masks–
Authentic leadership after crisis/failure

• The Achiever's Dilemma: When Success Feels Hollow–
For Enneagram Type 3s and high performers

Visit JustinZebell.com

WOULD YOU REVIEW THIS BOOK?

If you enjoyed reading *No Zero Days,* would you kindly take a few moments to leave a review wherever you purchased it (and perhaps even on Goodreads.com)? I'm grateful for your support. Thank you!

GRATITUDE

To my incredible girls who are the most important reflection of who I am. Each of you is so special, and no matter what the days ahead hold, I will always be in your corner. Girl dad for life!

To Anastasia, I could not be more proud of the young woman you are becoming. You have fought through adversity, surrounded yourself with great people, and chased your dreams in life. Keep chasing them; I am your biggest fan.

To Chloe, I've watched you blossom into an incredible young woman. You are wise for your age, a well-read thinker primed for leadership, and my TS bestie. I look forward to our *Minecraft* nights and I love each phase of life with you. I expect one day I will be reading your book or books as well.

To Claire, you exude joy to everyone around you. Your competitive fire and your "I got this" attitude will take you far in a life that is just beginning. I love our jokes and our snuggle times. I am honored that I get to train dragons with you and have a front row seat as you grow up.

To Anya, it has been a hard road, but through it all I love you and believe in you. If these last five years have taught me anything, it is that as long as we are breathing, there is always time for the comeback. I am always cheering for you.

To my mom, you did it. You raised me and taught me the value of unconditional love. Life wasn't always what you hoped for, I'm sure, but then as now, you spend your mornings and evenings praying for those around you. Your prayers for me and my family have had more impact than you'll ever know. We love you.

To Rex and Jeanene Russell, you have shown me the greatest example of love and given me a model to follow for my family. The girls absolutely adore you and thank you for taking us in as your own. I would not be where I am today without you.

To Madeline McDonald, God knew what He was doing when He brought you into our lives. You were here as part of His plan and I will be forever thankful. I am cheering you on each day. Let's go get these dreams!

To Jeff Helton, it has been almost fifteen years that I have been coming to your office off and on. You have no idea the difference you have made with the road map you gave me to follow. Thank you for never pounding me over the head with what I should do, but letting me get there on my own.

To Bill Reeves, that day in Starbucks you gave me perspective, permission to lean into the mess, and assurance that I could take my time coming out of it. Thank you for your friendship and your wisdom.

To Greg Ham, our regular breakfast meetings are often the highlight of my week. Watching you in each phase of life as you walk ahead of me in years … You inspire me both in family and in business.

To Bill Hampton, we have been a part of each other's circle, on and off, for nearly three decades. Your story and shared experiences came at a pivotal point for me in this journey. Thank you for your guidance along the way.

To Aaron Kinssies, we have covered a lot of miles and a lot of life. One of my greatest blessings has been truly reconnecting with lifelong friends, and I count you as one of those few. Thank you for always showing up and after all this time still making me laugh.

To Chad Landers, from tour buses to airports, to late-night ballrooms and phone calls, thank you. Thank you for being there as a friend first. We have both walked through some life together, and you showed grace even when I wasn't at my best.

To Mike Taylor, you showed me true friendship at a time I wasn't sure what that was. From Sunday football texts, to our sounding-board phone calls, to sharing a slice on occasion, I am truly thankful for you.

To Eric Brown, your life inspires me. You asked me one night after we left dinner, "How much did you lose?" In that moment I remember thinking that I'd lost nothing but money. Friendships like yours remind me that the community you speak of so often is all that matters. Thank you.

To Jennifer Cooke, thank you for your friendship amidst the chaos. From the very first time we met to the current day, we have done a lot together. Thank you for answering my phone calls and for supporting me through the years.

To Amy Grant, somewhere in the wreckage, I was reminded of many of our conversations over the years about the value of sitting still in the very moment God has placed you in. I watched you do this time and time again while the world buzzed around you, and I never fully understood it. I do now. Thank you for your friendship and for your investment in me, not just professionally, but as a human being. I look forward to our next life conversation at your house over coffee.

To Honorée Corder, we met at random over two years ago, and you have stayed with me through this entire process. You have championed me when I felt like an imposter in this experience of writing a book. I couldn't have done this without your patience and your encouragement along the way. Writing a book was nowhere on my radar five years ago, and I thank you greatly for pushing me to make this a reality.

To Alyssa Archer, you are a magician when it comes to taking my raw manuscript and moving it from good to great. From our first iteration to where we are today, I am in awe of your magic wand. Thank you for investing in this newbie author. This book is a reflection of great collaboration.

To Jesse Itzler, we have never met, but I, like thousands of others, have been inspired by your business and your family and the way you seem to manage both. For reasons that only God knows, He brought you to my social feed at the time I needed it most. And the words *No Zero Days* have impacted my life at a profound level and continue to do so today. Thank you for sharing your story and your life so openly with the public. Its reach extends far beyond what you can possibly imagine.

To my team, I have known some of you for almost a decade or more, and I speak a lot about the rebuild and what that takes. For each of you, it may be different, but for me, I know that it has been a team effort. It has been a privilege to watch each of you go through life's milestones, and no matter where the road takes us, you will always have someone to call—anytime, anyplace. Thank you.

WHO IS JUSTIN ZEBELL?

Justin Zebell is a founder, creator, and lifelong learner who has spent more than twenty-eight years at the intersection of business, creativity, and human experience. A natural entrepreneur, he's built multiple companies and led teams that have helped some of the world's leading brands tell their stories through unforgettable moments.

Through the highs of success and the lows of failure, Justin has discovered that the real lessons live in the hard seasons—that failure, more than success, shapes who we become. Today, he channels those lessons into new business ventures of his own, helping others build lives and companies rooted in purpose, resilience, and forward motion.

Whether leading companies, writing, or speaking, Justin is driven by one core belief: Progress happens one intentional day at a time. No Zero Days.

Above all, he's a proud father of four daughters, whose laughter, curiosity, and courage inspire the legacy he hopes to leave behind.